BIG
TRUTHS
FOR
LITTLE
KIDS

Teaching Your Children to Live for God

SUSAN HUNT & RICHIE HUNT

CROSSWAY BOOKS

A DIVISION OF
GOOD NEWS PUBLISHERS
WHEATON, ILLINOIS

To "The Cousins":

Hunter, Mary Kate, Daniel, Susie, and Sam Barriault

Cassie and Scotty Coley

Mac and Angus Hunt

With the prayer that whether they eat or drink or whatever they do,
they will do it all for the glory of God (1 Corinthians 10:31).

And to Gene, the granddaddy of them all.

And in memory of Annie Grace Barriault
who graced our family for eleven brief weeks.

I will utter hidden things, things from of old—

what we have heard and known, what our fathers have told us.

We will not hide them from their children;

we will tell the next generation

the praiseworthy deeds of the LORD,

his power, and the wonders he has done.

He decreed statutes for Jacob and established the law in Israel,

which he commanded our forefathers to teach their children,

so the next generation would know them,

even the children yet to be born,

and they in turn would tell their children.

Then they would put their trust in God

and would not forget his deeds

but would keep his commands.

PSALM 78:2-7

Big Truths for Little Kids

Copyright © 1999 by Susan Hunt and Richie Hunt

Published by Crossway Books
    a division of Good News Publishers
    1300 Crescent Street
    Wheaton, Illinois 60187

Cover design: Cindy Kiple

Illustration: Nancy Munger

First printing 1999

Printed in Thailand

Selected catechism questions and answers are quoted from *First Catechism—Biblical Truth for God's Children,* copyright © 1996 by Great Commission Publications, Inc. Used by permission. Contact at www.gcp.org or 800-595-3387.

Some material (designated "original edition") is reprinted from *Catechism for Young Children,* published by Christian Education and Publications, Presbyterian Church in America. Used by permission.

Scripture taken from the *Holy Bible: New International Version®.* Copyright © 1973, 1978, 1984 by International Bible Society. Used by permission of Zondervan Publishing House. All rights reserved.

The "NIV" and "New International Version" trademarks are registered in the United States Patent and Trademark Office by International Bible Society. Use of either trademark requires the permission of International Bible Society.

Scripture references marked NKJV are taken from the *New King James Version.* Copyright © 1982, Thomas Nelson, Inc. Used by permission.

The author may be contacred at PCA Christian Education and Publications. 1700 N. Brown Road. Lawrenceville, GA 30043. Phone : 678-825-1100.

LIBRARY OF CONGRESS CATALOGING-IN-PUBLICATION DATA
Hunt, Susan, 1940–
    Big truths for little kids : teaching your children to live for God /
Susan Hunt and Richie Hunt.
        p.   cm.
    ISBN 1-58134-106-7
    1. Catechisms, English. 2. Children—Religious life.
I. Hunt, Richie, 1967–   . II. Title.
BT1031.2.H86   1999
248.8'45—dc21   99-30536

IM									
	13	12	1	10	09	08	07	06	05
17	16	15	14	13	12	11	10	9	8

Dear Lover of Children:

Whether you are a parent, grandparent, teacher, or friend of the child you read to, thank you for sharing our passion to teach the next generation the praiseworthy deeds of our Lord. Our purpose for this book is:

• To teach children that they are created for God's glory.

• To show some practical implications of this life purpose.

• To repeatedly emphasize to children their need for God's grace to glorify Him.

These stories are an application of the truths taught in *First Catechism*. A catechism is simply a series of questions and answers that systematically teach a body of information. Catechizing children is an effective way to teach them a framework of biblical knowledge that helps them develop a Christian worldview. It is amazing how quickly children grasp the truths set before them and how quickly they begin to understand that how we live is based on what we believe.

One of our favorite stories is of a mom and dad who started teaching the catechism to their five-year-old son. To their surprise one night their three-year-old daughter said the answers. Another day the mother heard her little boy telling his friend that his daddy was at work. "Why does he go to work?" asked the friend. Without hesitation this little theologian answered, "For God's glory." That is a biblical perspective of life.

Love the Lord your God with all your heart and with all your soul and with all your strength. These commandments that I give you today are to be upon your hearts. Impress them on your children. Talk about them when you sit at home and when you walk along the road, when you lie down and when you get up.

DEUTERONOMY 6 : 5 - 7

For God's Glory,

Susan and Richie

P.S. from Richie: I grew up on the catechism. As we learned to talk, my sisters and I were taught the answers to the first few questions. As the Director of Children's Ministry at my church, one of my priorities is our catechism program. I want to share my rich inheritance with the kids in our church. Now I am grateful for the opportunity to share this legacy with the children you love.

P.S. from Susan: You can imagine my joy in working with our son on this project. Gene and I were committed to teaching the catechism to our children, so as we ate our meals, drove to soccer practice, and waited in orthodontist offices, we worked on the catechism. My frustration and discouragement at childish wiggling, resisting, and silliness has faded to a dim memory. Gene and I are thrilled that our children are teaching the catechism to the next generation. We pray that you will have the joy of seeing this fruit in the life of the child you love and teach.

How to Use This Book

We encourage you to help your child memorize the answers to the catechism questions. We suggest that the first time you read through this book, you set a goal of memorizing between five and fifteen answers, depending on the age of your child. Memorizing the entire catechism should be a long-term project. Repeatedly reading the stories will reinforce the application of biblical principles. A suggested procedure:

•Memorize the answers to the questions in story #1.

•Each day, as you move to a different story, begin by reviewing the questions for story #1. Then ask each question in the new story, say the answer, and ask the child to recite the answer with you. Do not try to memorize these answers.

•Read the story and discuss the questions.

•Review the questions for story #1 again.

•Once your child knows the answers to these first questions, add another question.

•Each time you read the book, memorize additional answers. The truths and the applications will be reinforced, and your child's understanding will expand.

•Whatever you do, have fun. Make this a special time with your child.

The "Let's Pray" section is designed to teach children to pray biblically. Read the verse, or let the child read it, and then use the very words of Scripture in your prayer. Soon your child will begin to use the language of Scripture as he or she prays.

Glorify the Lord with me; let us exalt his name together.

PSALM 34:3

Q. Who made you?

A. God

Q. What else did God make?

A. God made all things.

Q. Why did God make you and all things?

A. For His own glory.

Q. How can you glorify God?

A. By loving Him and doing what He commands.

Q. Why are you to glorify God?

A. Because He made me and takes care of me.

A Party at the Zoo

Cassie and Caleb love the Lord Jesus. Their mom and dad teach them about Jesus and take them to church so they can grow up in God's family. Every night Cassie and Caleb's parents ask them some questions about God. The children have been memorizing the questions and the answers. These questions and answers are from what is called the "catechism." After the children work on the catechism, then their parents pray that Cassie and Caleb will always glorify God in everything they do. They call Cassie and Caleb their "catechism kids."

A week before Caleb's eighth birthday, his mom said to him, "Caleb, we have a surprise for you. For your birthday we will take you to your favorite place—the zoo. And you may invite two friends. Whom would you like to ask?"

"Angus!" Caleb answered excitedly. "He's my best friend." Caleb and Angus were in the same Sunday school class.

"Who else do you want to invite?" asked his mom.

"I think I'll invite Daniel," said Caleb. "He doesn't have any friends yet." Daniel and his family had just moved next door to Caleb's family. Caleb's mom and dad had invited them to church, but they said they didn't go to church. Caleb continued, "Maybe if Daniel meets Angus, he'll want to go to Sunday school with me."

"That's a wonderful idea, Caleb," said his mom.

Finally it was the day of the party. After the boys arrived at Caleb's house, they watched

the birthday boy open the gifts they had given him. Angus gave Caleb a cool set of building blocks. Daniel gave him a new soccer ball. Then everyone piled in the van to go to the zoo.

The boys had a great time. They saw the giraffes and elephants. They went to the petting zoo and saw the chickens and goats and pigs. Then they went to see the monkeys. They laughed as they watched the monkeys climb and swing on the vines. "Just think," said Daniel, "we came from monkeys."

"What!" said Caleb and Angus at the same time. "We didn't evolve from monkeys. God created us," explained Caleb.

"What do you mean?" asked Daniel.

Angus replied, "The Bible says that God made everything. He made the world and the animals. Then He made the first people. God made everything."

"Are you sure?" asked Daniel. "I've never heard anything like that."

"We're sure," said Caleb and Angus with confidence.

Caleb added, "God made us for His own glory,

and He takes care of us."

"Really?" asked Daniel. "How do you know all of that?"

"The Bible tells us about God," replied Angus.

"Why don't you come to church with me tomorrow?" asked Caleb. "It's really cool, and we learn a lot about God."

"You would like our Sunday school class," said Angus.

"I'll ask Mom and Dad if I can go," replied Daniel as the three boys ran to see a peacock that had just spread out his beautiful feathers.

Let's talk

1. Tell the story back to me. What are the names of the brother and sister, and what do their parents call them? What happened in the story?

2. What did Caleb and Angus explain to Daniel?

3. Why did God make you and all things?

Let's pray

Do you not know? Have you not heard? The LORD is the everlasting God, the Creator of the ends of the earth. He will not grow tired or weary, and his understanding no one can fathom. (ISAIAH 40:28)

Thank God for what you learn about Him in this verse.

Q. Are there more Gods than one?

A. There is only one true God.

Q. In how many persons is this one true God?

A. Three.

Q. Name these three persons.

A. The Father, the Son, and the Holy Spirit.

Q. What is God?

A. God is a Spirit and has no body as we do.

Q. Where is God?

A. God is everywhere.

Daniel Goes to Church

Caleb and Angus prayed that Daniel's parents would let him go to church with them on Sunday. They were excited when Daniel said he could go. Then they started praying that Daniel would like church and that he would learn about Jesus.

Everyone in the Sunday school class was nice to Daniel. Caleb and Angus let Daniel sit between them, even though they really liked sitting next to each other.

On the way home from church, Daniel said, "I liked church. That story about Daniel in the lion's den was about the best story I've ever heard. Is that a true story?"

"Yes, Daniel," explained Caleb's dad. "That story is in the Bible. The Bible is God's Word, and every word is true."

"Daniel was so brave!" said Daniel. "He must have been a superhero."

Caleb's dad smiled and said, "Well, actually Daniel was brave because of what he knew about God and because God gave him grace to obey. The best part about that story is not Daniel's bravery but God's faithfulness to His children. You see, God is sovereign. That means He is everywhere, He is all-powerful, and He is in charge of

everything that happens. So He could protect the Daniel in the Bible *and* the Daniel in the backseat of our car."

"Cool," said Daniel. "I'm glad I'm learning about God."

Then the boys started talking about soccer. The next day they would find out which team they would be on. "I hope I get on the same team with you and Angus," said Daniel. Caleb and Angus had been on the same team every year since they started playing soccer, and they were pretty sure they would be on the same team again. But on Monday, when the boys got to the soccer field and the coaches read the names on each team, Angus and

Daniel were on the red team, and Caleb was on the green team.

"That's not fair," said Daniel angrily. "You should be on the team with us. We asked to be on the same team."

Caleb was really disappointed, but he remembered what he had learned about God. He knew that God is everywhere, so God had been there when it was decided who would be on each team. He prayed silently in his heart, "Dear God, help me to trust You and to be a good sport."

"It's okay, Daniel," Caleb said. "God is in charge. He put me on the team He wants me to be on. I want to be on the team with you and Angus, but the most important thing is to be where God wants me to be and to glorify Him."

"Wow," said Daniel. "Being a Christian is pretty cool."

Let's talk

1. What are some things you learn about God from these catechism answers and from this story?

2. Why wasn't Caleb angry about not being on the same team with Angus and Daniel?

3. What is the word that tells us that God is everywhere, that He is all powerful and that He is in charge of everything?

Let's pray

How great You are, O Sovereign Lord! There is no one like you, and there is no God but you. (2 SAMUEL 7:22)

Thank God for what you learn about Him in this verse.

Q. Can you see God?

A. No, I cannot see God, but He can always see me.

Q. Does God know all things?

A. Yes. Nothing can be hidden from God.

Q. Can God do all things?

A. Yes. God can do all His holy will.

The Tree House

For weeks Caleb, Angus, and Daniel talked about building a tree house in Angus's backyard. But the boys did not have any wood.

"If we had a tree house, we could pretend it was our fort, and we could battle the bad guys!" Angus said.

"If we only had some wood," the boys all said together.

One day Daniel ran into Angus's backyard pulling his wagon filled with wood! And it was not just any old wood. It was really good wood—perfect for the tree house.

"This is great!" exclaimed Caleb.

"Yeah. Now we can build our tree house," said Angus.

The three boys immediately started planning. "Maybe we can lay some boards across these limbs," suggested Daniel.

"I'll go get a hammer and some nails from my dad's workshop," said Angus.

"This is great—this is really great. Say, Daniel, where did you get all this wood anyway?" asked Caleb.

"I got it where those men are building that new house," Daniel told them.

"Wow. That was really nice of those men to give you all this wood," said Angus.

Daniel looked up from his work and said, "Well, they didn't really give it to me. They left for lunch, and I just took some. They've got so much wood stacked up there that they won't miss a few pieces."

Caleb and Angus looked at each other, and then they looked at Daniel. Angus said,

"We can't keep this."

"What do you mean, we can't keep it?" protested Daniel. "Nobody saw me, and those men have so much they'll never miss it."

"God saw you, and it's stealing," replied Angus firmly.

"Last night in our family devotions my dad read us some verses from Psalm 33. I think we need to read those verses now," said Caleb. He ran to his house and quickly returned with his Bible. Caleb read: "From heaven the Lord looks down and sees all mankind; from his dwelling place he watches all who live on earth" (Psalm 33:13-14).

Daniel listened intently and then said, "Oh no. Those men didn't see me, but God saw me, didn't He?"

Caleb and Angus nodded. "Come on, Daniel, let's load up the wood. We'll go with you to return it to the men," Angus offered.

"I'll tell the men that I'm sorry, and I think I need to tell God I'm sorry too," said Daniel. The boys bowed their heads and Daniel asked the Lord to forgive him. He also asked the Lord to give him courage to tell the men he was sorry.

As the boys walked down the street, Daniel said, "It's scary knowing that God sees everything we do."

Angus replied, "But wouldn't it be scarier if God didn't see us? Then He couldn't take care of us."

"Yeah—that's right," Daniel agreed.

"And God loves us, even when we do bad things," said Caleb.

Angus looked thoughtful for a moment. Then he spoke. "You know, Daniel, I think it's really cool that you're willing to take the wood back. God saw you when you took the wood, but He also sees you now."

"Yeah," Caleb chimed in. "It seems to me that you're glorifying God because you're doing the right thing now."

Let's talk

1. What did the boys want to build?

2. What did Daniel do that was wrong?

3. Who saw Daniel steal the wood?

4. Why did God make you and all things?

5. How did Daniel glorify God?

Let's pray

From heaven the Lord looks down and sees all mankind; from his dwelling place he watches all who live on earth. (PSALM 33:13-14)

Thank God for what you learn about Him in this verse.

Q. Where do you learn how to love and obey God?

A. In the Bible alone.

Q. Who wrote the Bible?

A. Chosen men who wrote by the inspiration of the Holy Spirit.

Daniel's Spiritual Birthday

Sunday morning is sleep-in time for Daniel's parents. Daniel is only eight years old, but every Saturday night he sets his alarm clock so he can get up on Sunday morning and go to church with Caleb and his family. It's Daniel's favorite day of the week. He loves church, and he loves learning about Jesus.

One Sunday Mr. Grant, the Sunday school teacher, said, "I know that many of you do not remember a time when you did not love Jesus. You believe that He died to pay for your sins, and you trust Him to be your Savior. Some of you do remember the time when you asked Jesus to forgive your sins and to be your Savior. But if there is anyone here who is not sure you are a Christian, and you want to talk about it, I encourage you to talk with me or with someone else."

Daniel immediately raised his hand. "Mr. Grant, I want to be a Christian," he said earnestly. "Sometimes I think I'll bust, I want to be a Christian so much."

"Daniel," said Mr. Grant, "I've been praying that God's Holy Spirit would teach you His Word and bring you to Himself. This is an answer to prayer."

Daniel went to the front of the room, stood beside Mr. Grant, and prayed, asking Jesus to forgive his sin and to be his Savior. Then Mr. Grant asked Caleb and Angus to pray for Daniel. Caleb thanked God for saving Daniel. Angus asked the Lord to help Daniel to glorify God.

Mr. Grant opened his Bible and said, "Boys and girls, Proverbs 30:5 says, 'Every word of God is flawless. . . .' That means there are no mistakes. The Bible is not like any other book. It is inspired. That means God chose men to write the words, but He told them exactly what He wanted them to say."

Mr. Grant turned the pages of his Bible and read: "All Scripture is God-breathed and is useful for teaching, rebuking, correcting and training in righteousness, so that the man of God may be thoroughly equipped for every good work" (2 Timothy 3:16-17).

Then Mr. Grant thanked God for His

inspired Word. He thanked God that the Holy Spirit had given Daniel a new heart so he could understand the Bible and realize his need for a Savior. He prayed that Daniel would always read God's Word and grow up to be a man of God ready to do every good work.

After Sunday school Caleb and Daniel could hardly wait to tell Caleb's parents what had happened. On the way home from church, Caleb's dad said, "Daniel, today is your spiritual birthday. Today you were born into God's family. What a special day for you and for us."

The car stopped in front of Daniel's house, and as soon as Daniel was out of the car, Cassie said, "I have a great idea! Dad, you said this is Daniel's spiritual birthday. I think we should get him a birthday present."

"That is a great idea, Cassie," said her mom. "What should we get for Daniel?"

"I know what Daniel wants more than anything else," said Caleb. "He wants a Bible of his very own."

The next day Cassie and Caleb went with their mom to buy a Bible for Daniel. They had his name and the date of his spiritual birthday printed on the cover.

Tears filled Daniel's eyes when he opened his gift. He hugged his new Bible and said, "Thank you, thank you. Now I can read God's Word and learn more about Him."

God had many wonderful plans for that Bible, but we will hear more about that later.

Let's talk

1. What happened in this story?

2. Why is the Bible such a special book?

3. Where do we learn how to glorify God?

Let's pray

Your hands made me and formed me; give me understanding to learn your commands.

(PSALM 119:73)

Make this your prayer.

Q. Who were the first people?

A. Adam and Eve.

Q. How did God make the first people?

A. God made Adam's body out of the ground and Eve's body out of a rib from Adam.

Q. What did God give Adam and Eve besides bodies?

A. He gave them spirits that will last forever.

Q. Do you have a spirit as well as a body?

A. Yes, and my spirit is going to last forever.

Q. How do you know your spirit will last forever?

A. Because the Bible tells me so.

Q. In what condition did God make Adam and Eve?

A. He made them holy and happy.

Which Bear Will It Be?

Cassie squealed with delight when she opened the letter addressed to her. It was an invitation to Mary Kate's birthday party. The invitation read:

You are invited to a Teddy Bear Tea Party.

Come and bring your favorite teddy bear.

Every day Cassie set all of her teddy bears in a line and asked herself, "Which bear should I take?" Should she take her Pooh Bear, her beautiful Victorian bear, her cuddly Baby Bear, or her all-time favorite—Teddy Mac?

Finally one day she announced, "I have made a decision."

"Well, Cassie, which bear will it be?" asked her mother.

"I'm going to take Teddy Mac. I know he's not the most beautiful. He's ragged and worn. But I love him. I think I'll put a bright bow around his neck for the party."

Cassie's grandfather, whom she called Papa Mac, had given her this bear for her third birthday. The family loved to tell the story of how Cassie opened the box, saw the bear, flung her arms around it, and said, "I *love* you." Then she ran to her grandfather, hugged him, and said, "Thank you, Papa Mac, for Teddy Mac." The whole family collapsed in laughter, and the bear became known as Teddy Mac.

"Mom," said Cassie with a worried look, "will the other girls make fun of Teddy Mac because he is ragged? I don't want them to hurt his feelings."

Cassie's mom sat down and put Cassie in her lap. "I think we need to talk," she said.

"Cassie, I know you love Teddy Mac, just as you love your dog and your fish. But toys and animals are not like people. They don't think and feel and love as we do. When God made people, He made us very special. He gave us something that toys and animals do not have. God gave us a spirit that will last forever. When we become Christians, God's Holy Spirit gives us the power to love God and worship Him. God's Holy Spirit also gives us power to love one another. People are made in God's image. We can glorify God by loving Him and doing what He commands in the Bible. If the girls laugh at Teddy Mac, it will hurt you, but it won't hurt him. But I don't think your friends will laugh. I think if you tell them why Teddy Mac is your favorite, they will love you even more."

On the day of the party, Cassie put on her pretty yellow dress, and her mother helped her put a big yellow bow around Teddy Mac's neck. They wrapped Mary Kate's gift with yellow paper and put another yellow bow on it. When Mary Kate opened the gift, she exclaimed, "Oh, Cassie, I love it, and I love you and Teddy Mac! I'm so glad you brought Teddy Mac to my party."

The gift was a teddy bear picture frame with a picture of Mary Kate and Cassie when they were four years old. In the picture, they were having a tea party, and both girls were serving Teddy Mac *pretend* tea and cookies.

Let's talk

1. Who were the first people?

2. What did God give Adam and Eve besides bodies?

3. How are we different from animals?

4. How can you glorify God?

Let's pray

For you created my inmost being; you knit me together in my mother's womb. I praise you because I am fearfully and wonderfully made; your words are wonderful, I know that full well. (PSALM 139:13-14)

Thank God for what you learn in this verse.

Q. What is a sacred covenant?

A. A relationship that God sets up with us and guarantees by His word.

Q. What covenant did God make with Adam?

A. The covenant of life.

Q. What did God require Adam to do in the covenant of life?

A. To obey Him perfectly.

Q. What did God promise in the covenant of life?

A. To reward Adam with life if he obeyed Him.

Q. What did God threaten in the covenant of life?

A. To punish Adam with death if he disobeyed Him.

Q. Did Adam keep the covenant of life?

A. No. He sinned against God.

Daniel Spends the Night

Daniel was spending the night with Caleb. Caleb's home was different from his own because after dinner they had family devotions. They sang songs, Caleb's mom or dad read a story, they learned a catechism answer, and then they all prayed. On this particular night, this is the story Caleb's dad read:

When God made Adam and Eve, He made them in His own image. He gave them a beautiful place to live. The wonder and the glory of that place was that God came each day and visited them. He talked to them. They knew Him in a personal way.

Adam and Eve lived in the presence of God's glory, and they showed His glory to each other. They were not selfish. They treated each other the way God treated them. Adam and Eve did not deserve to have this special friendship with God. They had not earned the right to live in His

presence. But God made them in His image so they could know and love Him.

God made an agreement with Adam and Eve. He gave them all the fruit of the garden to eat, but He told them not to eat from the Tree of the Knowledge of Good and Evil. God promised that if they obeyed Him, they could continue to live in His presence. If they disobeyed, they would die. This is called the covenant of life.

A covenant is an agreement that must not be broken.

Then one day Satan came to Eve and said, "Did God really say you must not eat from any tree in the garden? You will not die if you eat from that tree. If you eat it, you will be like God."

Eve listened to Satan. She took the fruit, and she gave some to Adam. They chose to disobey God. They chose not to live under God's authority. They sinned.

God came to the garden. He told Adam and Eve that they had to leave. They could not live in His presence because of their sin.

Caleb's dad noticed that Daniel looked very sad. "Daniel, are you all right?" he asked.

"I wish God would let Adam and Eve back in the garden," said Daniel.

"Oh, Daniel," said Caleb's mom. "The Good News is that God did make a way for Adam and Eve, and for us, to live in His presence. God sent Jesus to die on the cross for our sin so that we will not be separated from Him."

"Do you mean that one day I will live in God's presence since Jesus is my Savior?" asked Daniel.

"Daniel, you don't have to wait to live in God's presence. You live in the light of God's presence *now*. We know Him. We love Him. We talk to Him in prayer. He talks to us through His Word. His Spirit lives in us. That's part of what it means to live in His presence. And when we go to heaven, we will live in the *fullness* of His presence," said Caleb's dad.

"Wow," said Daniel. "I sure am glad I live in God's presence. Can we pray that my mom and dad will ask Jesus to be their Savior so they can live in God's presence?"

"Yes, Daniel. And let's ask the Lord to give you grace to show God's glory to your mom and dad."

Let's talk

1. What was Daniel's favorite thing about spending the night at Caleb's house?

2. What did you learn from the story Caleb's dad told?

3. Why was Daniel sad when he heard the story of Adam and Eve?

4. What did Caleb's mom explain to Daniel?

Let's pray

For all have sinned and fall short of the glory of God. (ROMANS 3:23)

For the wages of sin is death, but the gift of God is eternal life in Christ Jesus our Lord. (ROMANS 6:23)

Thank God for what you learn in these verses.

Q. What is sin?

A. Any thought, word, or deed that breaks God's law by omission or commission.

Q. What is a sin of omission?

A. Not being or doing what God requires.

Q. What is a sin of commission?

A. Doing what God forbids.

Q. What does every sin deserve?

A. The wrath and curse of God.

Truth Time

Caleb, Angus, and Daniel made a pact. They agreed to read their Bibles every day and to learn the memory verse from their Sunday school lesson each week.

"I have an idea," said Caleb. "Let's meet every Saturday afternoon in my tent and say our memory verse to each other and tell each other if we read our Bibles every day."

"Yeah," said Angus. "It's like a covenant, because we all agree to tell each other the truth."

"Let's call it Truth Time," suggested Daniel.

The boys gave each other high fives as they said together, "Truth Time!"

On Saturday the boys met. Their memory verse was Ephesians 6:1: "Children, obey your parents in the Lord, for this is right."

Each of the boys said they had read their Bible every day. Then each one said the memory verse. "Now let's play soccer!" said Caleb.

"Wait a minute, guys," said Daniel. "We said this is Truth Time, and I don't think I have been truthful."

"What do you mean?" asked Angus.

"Well," said Daniel, "I read my Bible, and I memorized the verse, but I didn't do what the verse says. There were lots of times this week when I thought bad things about my parents and said ugly things to them. There were lots of times when I didn't obey my par-

ents. Is this what the catechism means when it says that sin is any thought, word, or deed that breaks God's law? What am I supposed to do when I sin? Does this mean I'm not a Christian anymore?"

"I don't know," said Caleb. "This is *big*. I think we need my dad. Wait just a minute."

Soon Caleb was back with his dad and his Bible. "I'm thankful that you boys are asking some very important questions," said Caleb's dad. "Daniel, you were not saved by being good. You were saved by God's grace. We cannot be good enough to earn salvation. Our sin *deserves* God's wrath and curse, but He gives us what we do not deserve. He gives us Jesus. He gave you a new heart so that you could believe that Jesus died for your sins. You will still sin, but your new heart will be bothered when you sin. Daniel, how did you feel when you disobeyed your parents?"

"I felt yucky inside," said Daniel. "I knew it was wrong, and I kept thinking about the memory verse, but I didn't know what to do."

Caleb's dad smiled. "Daniel, I'm glad you felt yucky because that shows that the Holy Spirit is working in your heart. The Holy Spirit was reminding you of God's

Word. Now listen to a wonderful promise that God makes to Christians." Caleb's dad opened his Bible and read I John 1:9: "If we confess our sins, he is faithful and just and will forgive us our sins and purify us from all unrighteousness."

"Boys, when you sin, you must quickly confess your sins to God and ask Him to forgive you. You must also ask Him for grace to obey His Word. And when you sin against someone else, you must ask that person to forgive you. Daniel, we have been praying that your parents will see God's glory in you. Why don't you ask them to forgive you for disobeying them? That will be an amazing testimony of God's grace in you."

Let's Talk

1. What is sin?

2. What does our sin deserve?

3. What did you learn from this story?

4. What should we do when we sin?

Let's Pray

For it is by grace you have been saved, through faith—and this not from yourselves, it is the gift of God—not by works, so that no one can boast. (EPHESIANS 2:8-9)

Thank God for His grace. Ask Him for grace to glorify Him in your thoughts, words, and actions.

Q. What was the sin of our first parents?

A. Eating the forbidden fruit.

Q. Who tempted them to this sin?

A. Satan tempted Eve first, and then he used her to tempt Adam.

Q. How did Adam and Eve change when they sinned?

A. Instead of being holy and happy, they became sinful and miserable.

Q. Did Adam act for himself alone in the covenant of life?

A. No. He represented the whole human race.

Cassie Learns to Encourage Others

Cassie loved playing soccer, but she was not a very good player. "Maybe I should just quit," Cassie said one night during dinner. "They would be better off if they didn't have me on the team."

"Cassie, let's think about this," urged her dad. "Do you like playing soccer?"

"Yes," replied Cassie excitedly. "I love everyone on my team, and I like being part of the team, but I know I'm not a good player."

"Don't quit, Cassie," said Caleb kindly. "I'll practice with you and help you."

Mom and Dad smiled. They were thankful that Caleb wanted to help his sister.

"Cassie, I want you to listen carefully," said her dad. "You can give something very important to your team. There is at least one thing that you can do better than anyone else."

Cassie was surprised. "What is it? I'm not a fast runner, I can't pass the ball, and I stumble when I try to dribble."

Her dad said, "Cassie, every team needs an encourager. Every team needs someone who helps the team to

work as a team and not just as a lot of individuals. You said that you love the girls on your team, and you love being a part of the team. Why don't you ask God for grace not to be jealous of the girls who are good players? Let's pray that God will give you grace to be an encourager to your team."

Many afternoons Caleb practiced with Cassie. Every night Cassie's family prayed for her. They asked God to give her grace to encourage others. An amazing thing happened. Cassie stopped worrying so much about not being a good player. She began to think more about her team.

At practices she worked hard to improve her game, and she tried to encourage the other girls. She never complained when the coach told them to run another lap. At the games Cassie never sat on the bench and sulked. She cheered for her team the whole time. When someone made a good play, Cassie was the first to give her a high five and say, "Good job!" And when someone missed a goal, Cassie comforted her: "That's okay—we'll get it next time."

At the end of the season, Cassie's team had won enough games to be in the citywide tournament. At practice the coach said, "I have an important announcement. At the first game of the tournament, all of the teams are going to be on the field for the opening ceremonies. Each coach is to select one player to represent our team and carry a flag with the name of our team. You have all been great players, and you have all improved tremendously. But there is one person we could not do without, not because she is our best player but because she has helped everyone else to be the best she can be. She has been cooperative. She has been a good sport. She has been an encourager. I have decided that Cassie should represent our team."

Everyone clapped. "Yea, Cassie," they shouted. The other girls all hugged her.

That night at dinner Cassie's family talked about how exciting it was that Cassie would represent her team.

"That makes me think about Adam representing us in the covenant of life," said Cassie's dad.

"But, Cassie, don't blow it like Adam did," Caleb teased.

Everyone laughed, and then Cassie's dad said, "Cassie, remember that Adam is not the only one who represented us. Jesus represented us in the covenant of grace, and it is because of God's grace in you that you have shown a Christlike character to your soccer team. Jesus represented us in the covenant of grace so that we can live in God's presence and so we can have His power to show His character to others. Cassie, God has given you grace to glorify Him. We pray that you will always glorify Him in everything you do."

Let's Talk

1. Why did Cassie want to quit playing soccer?

2. What did her dad tell her that she could do?

3. What was Cassie chosen to do?

4. How did Cassie glorify God?

5. Who represented us in the covenant of life?

6. Who represented us in the covenant of grace?

Let's Pray

So whether you eat or drink or whatever you do, do it all for the glory of God. (1 CORINTHIANS 10:31)

Ask God for grace to glorify Him in everything you do.

Q. What did Adam's sin do to you?

A. It made me guilty and sinful.

Q. How sinful are you by nature?

A. I am corrupt in every part of my being.

Q. Can you go to heaven with this sinful nature?

A. No. My heart must be changed before I can be fit for heaven.

Q. What is the changing of your heart called?

A. The new birth, or regeneration.

Q. Who is able to change your heart?

A. The Holy Spirit alone.

A New Heart

Good morning, Daniel," said Caleb's dad as Daniel ran across the yard and piled into the car with their family. "We are so thankful that you go to church with us every Sunday."

"Sunday is my favorite day," said Daniel. "I love going to church. But I wish my mom and dad would go with us."

"I don't understand why they don't want to go," said Cassie.

"Let's think about that," said her dad as he backed the car out of the drive. "Why do you and I want to go to church?"

"Because we love Jesus and we want to worship Him," said Cassie.

"But *why* do we know and love Jesus? *Why* do we want to worship Him? Are we better or smarter than people who do not know and love Jesus?" asked her dad.

"Well," said Caleb thoughtfully, "I know we are not better or smarter. I think it's because we have new hearts."

"That's right, Caleb," said his dad. "But *why* do you have a new heart when someone else does not? Did you just decide one day to ask Jesus to give you a new heart?"

"Wow," said Cassie. "I don't know."

"I never thought about it before," said Caleb.

"You see, kids, the Bible says that we are dead in sin. That doesn't mean that our bodies are dead. What part is dead?"

"Our spirits?"

"Right—the part of us that we can't see. Now what can a dead person do?" asked their dad.

"Nothing!" they exclaimed.

"That's right," their dad replied. "A spiritually dead person can't do anything spiritual. We can't *understand* that we are sinners and need a Savior. We can't *believe* that Jesus is the Savior. God has to do something for us so that we can believe. Daniel, look up Ezekiel 36:26-27 in your Bible. Cassie, look up Deuteronomy 7:7-9. Caleb, you look up Ephesians 2."

The sound of turning pages filled the car. Then Daniel said, "Ezekiel 36:26-27: 'I will give you a new heart and put a new spirit in you; I will remove from you your heart of stone and give you a heart of flesh. And I will put my Spirit in you and move you to follow my decrees and be careful to keep my laws.'"

Caleb's dad said, "God is speaking in these verses. He is telling us that *He* will give us a new heart that will love and obey him. This is called the new birth, or regeneration. This is what it means to be born again. Now the question that I always think about is: 'Why would God give *me* a new heart?' Cassie, read your verse."

Cassie read, "Deuteronomy 7:7-9: 'The LORD did not set his affection on you and choose you because you were more numerous than other peoples, for you were the fewest of all peoples. But it was because the LORD loved you. . . . Know therefore that the LORD your God is God; he is the faithful God, keeping his covenant of love to a thousand generations of those who love him and keep his commands.'"

"You see, kids," said their dad, "there is nothing about us that causes God to give us a new heart so we can know and love Him. It is because of His love. It is because of His covenant of grace. Now, Caleb, read Ephesians 2:1, then verses 4 and 5."

Caleb read: "'As for you, you were dead in your transgressions and sins. . . . But because of his great love for us, God, who is rich in mercy, made us alive with Christ even when we were dead in transgressions—it is by grace you have been saved.'"

"Now let's all say Ephesians 2:8-9 together." As they drove into the church parking lot, they all said, "'For it is by grace you have been saved, through faith—and this not from yourselves, it is the gift of God—not by works, so that no one can boast.'"

Let's Talk

1. Adam represented us in the covenant of life. When he sinned, what did this do to us?

2. Do you believe in Jesus because you are smarter or better than other people? What did you learn from this story?

3. Who gives us a new heart so we can believe in Jesus and glorify God?

Let's Pray

For it is by grace you have been saved, through faith—and this not from yourselves, it is the gift of God—not by works, so that no one can boast. (EPHESIANS 2:8-9)

Thank God for His grace. Ask Him for grace to glorify Him in your thoughts, words, and actions.

Q. Can you be saved through the covenant of life?

A. No, because I broke it and am condemned by it.

Q. How did you break the covenant of life?

A. Adam represented me, and so I fell with him in his first sin.

Q. How, then, can you be saved?

A. By the Lord Jesus Christ in the covenant of grace.

Q. Who was represented by Jesus in the covenant of grace?

A. His elect people.

Q. How did Jesus fulfill the covenant of grace?

A. He kept the whole law for his people and then was punished for all of their sins.

A Baby Sister

Cassie was walking down the church hallway to her Sunday school class when she heard someone call, "Cassie, wait. I have something important to tell you." She turned and saw her friend Susie coming toward her as fast as she could walk without breaking into a run. One look at Susie's face told Cassie that something exciting was going on.

"Cassie, you will never guess what's going to happen!" Susie exclaimed breathlessly. Without waiting for Cassie to guess, Susie blurted out, "My mom's going to have a baby!"

"Wow! Oh, Susie, I'm so excited for you!" exclaimed Cassie as she hugged Susie. Both girls tried hard to keep from squealing and jumping and making a spectacle of themselves. Running and squealing and jumping would be disrespectful and inappropriate in church.

"The doctor said that the baby is a girl," said Susie. "I have always wanted a baby sister. And we already know what we are going to name her."

"A baby sister—oh, Susie, what fun! What is her name?"

Susie now had settled down and sounded very grown-up as she explained, "Mom and Dad have named all of us for someone in our family. I'm named for my great-grand-mother. Mom said that this baby will be named Annie Grace. Well, I could understand nam-ing her Annie because that is my grandmother's name, but I didn't know why we would name a baby Grace. But Mom said, 'We are saved by God's grace, we live by His grace, we are in His family because of His grace. So Grace really is a family name.' Dad said that Annie Grace will remind us of God's amazing grace that we don't deserve."

"Susie, I love that name," said Cassie. "It makes me think about our memory verse."

Both girls recited the verse together: "Ephesians 2:8-9: 'For it is by grace you have been saved, through faith—and this not from yourselves, it is the gift of God—not by works, so that no one can boast.'"

Just then their Sunday school teacher, Mrs. Thompson, walked up. "Well, girls, I'm glad to hear you practicing your memory verse." Susie told her the exciting news, and Mrs. Thompson said, "Susie, I think you should share this with the entire class."

After Susie told the class about the baby, Mrs. Thompson said, "Boys and girls, this baby is a covenant child that the Lord is giving to Susie's family and to our church family. Her name can remind us all that grace is God's love that we do not deserve and cannot earn. Grace is a gift. We should begin right now to pray for Annie Grace. What do you think we should pray for her?"

"That she will love Jesus," said Megan.

"My mom prays for the man I will marry and for my children," said Cassie. "I think we should pray for Annie Grace's husband and children and that she will have a Christian family."

"I think we should pray that she will glorify God in everything she does," said Susie.

Now Mrs. Thompson could hardly control herself. She wanted to squeal and jump and make a spectacle of herself because she was so thrilled that the boys and girls in her class were so full of God's grace.

Let's Talk

1. Why was Susie so excited?

2. What did Susie's mom and dad decide to name the new baby?

3. Why did they want to name her Grace?

4. What did the boys and girls want to pray for this new baby?

Let's Pray

For it is by grace you have been saved, through faith—and this not from yourselves, it is the gift of God—not by works, so that no one can boast. (EPHESIANS 2:8-9)

Thank God for His grace. Ask Him for grace to glorify Him in your thoughts, words, and actions.

Q. Did Jesus ever sin?

A. No. He lived a sinless life.

Q. How could the Son of God suffer?

A. The Son of God became a man so that He could obey and suffer.

Q. For whom did Christ obey and suffer?

A. For all who were given to Him by the Father.

Q. What kind of life did Christ live on earth?

A. A life of poverty and suffering.

Q. What kind of death did Jesus die?

A. The painful and shameful death of the cross.

Daniel's New Bible

Daniel loved the Bible Cassie and Caleb gave him for his spiritual birthday. "Daniel," said Caleb's dad, "I encourage you to read God's Word every day. Why don't you begin by reading the Gospel of John."

Daniel started reading that very night. He liked to sit in his bed and read before he went to sleep. But there was a problem. When he finished reading, he had to get out of bed to turn the light off. Many nights he finished reading and fell asleep with the light still on. "I have a solution," said his mom. "We'll get a reading lamp for your bed."

Daniel felt quite grown-up having a reading lamp. Now he could read, turn the light off, snuggle under his covers, and never have to get out of bed. One night Daniel came to chapter 19 in the book of John. He read:

Then Pilate took Jesus and had him flogged. The soldiers twisted together a crown of thorns and put it on his head. They clothed him in a purple robe and went up to him again and again, saying, "Hail, king of the Jews!" And they struck him in the face.

"That's awful," said Daniel. He continued reading, and soon he came to these words:

As soon as the chief priests and their officials saw him, they shouted, "Crucify! Crucify!" But Pilate answered, "You take him and crucify him. As for me, I find no basis for a charge against him."

"That's right! Jesus didn't do anything wrong. He never sinned," Daniel said.

Then a few verses later he read:

Finally Pilate handed him over to them to be crucified. So the soldiers took charge of Jesus. Carrying his own

cross, he went out to the place of the Skull (which in Aramaic is called Golgotha). Here they crucified him . . .

"Oh no," Daniel groaned. "It must have been terrible for Jesus to hang on that cross. I guess this is what the catechism means when it says 'the painful and shameful death of the cross'."

Then Daniel came to these words:

Near the cross of Jesus stood his mother. . . . When Jesus saw his mother there, and the disciple whom he loved standing nearby, he said to his mother, "Dear woman, here is your son," and to the disciple, "Here is your mother." From that time on, this disciple took her into his home.

"Jesus was so poor that he didn't even have a house for his mother," Daniel said sadly. "How kind of Him to think about her when He was in so much pain."

Then he read:

Jesus said, "It is finished." With that, he bowed his head and gave up his spirit."

Daniel began to cry. His mother came into the room. "Daniel, what's wrong?"

"I was just reading about Jesus dying on the cross for me. He loves me so much that He died for my sin," said Daniel.

"Daniel," said his mom, "I'm not sure I like you reading this Bible if it's going to make you cry."

"Oh no, Mom," said Daniel quickly. "It makes me sad to know that Jesus hung on the cross for me, but that's not the end of the story. Jesus came back alive. He's alive now. Listen to what He said before He died." Daniel quickly turned to John 14. He smiled as he read:

"Do not let your hearts be troubled. Trust in God; trust also in me. In my Father's house are many rooms; if it were not so, I would have told you. I am going there to prepare a place for you. And if I go and prepare a place for you, I will come back and take you to be with me that you also may be where I am."

"Daniel," said his mom, "I don't understand what's happening to you. But I do know that you are kinder and more obedient. I guess it's okay for you to keep reading your Bible and going to church. But I don't like for you to be sad."

"I love you, Mom," said Daniel.

"And I love you, Daniel," she said as she leaned over and kissed him good night.

Daniel turned off his light, snuggled under his covers, and prayed, "Jesus, thank You for dying for me. Please help Mom to understand, and help me to be kind to her like You were to Your mother."

Let's Talk

1. What did you learn from this story?

2. How does it make you feel to think about Jesus dying for you?

3. How do you feel when you read about Jesus preparing a place for you in heaven?

Let's Pray

For you know the grace of our Lord Jesus Christ, that though he was rich, yet for your sakes he became poor, so that you through his poverty might become rich. (2 CORINTHIANS 8:9)

Thank God for what you learn in this verse.

Q. What is meant by the atonement?

A. Christ satisfied God's justice by His suffering and death in the place of sinners.

Q. What did God the Father guarantee in the covenant of grace?

A. To justify and sanctify all those for whom Christ died.

Oops!

Cassie and Caleb were practicing soccer in their backyard. Caleb was helping Cassie learn to kick the ball.

A fence stretched between their yard and the yard behind them. They had been told not to kick the ball in that direction because their neighbors had a beautiful garden with very expensive birdhouses collected from all over the world. Mr. and Mrs. Nelson loved to have the neighborhood children visit them. They even had parties and invited children to come and learn about flowers and birds.

Cassie and Caleb were not paying attention to the direction they were facing. And frankly Caleb was not too concerned because he didn't think Cassie could ever kick the ball that far. That was when it happened. After what seemed to be a zillion attempts, Cassie ran up to the ball, kicked as hard as she could, and that ball flew through the air and over the fence. The next thing they heard was the sound of wood crashing to the ground. They froze.

Finally Caleb said slowly, "Oh no."

Cassie's voice was filled with dread. "Caleb, what have I done?" They walked slowly to the fence. When they peeked over, their hearts sank. A prized hand-carved birdhouse from Germany had fallen onto a concrete bench. It looked like a pile of splinters. Tears streamed down Cassie's face.

Caleb gently took her hand, and the two of them walked back to their house in silence. They knew what they had to do. Their mom and dad in the kitchen took one look at their children's faces and knew something was wrong.

"I'm so sorry. I've done a terrible thing, and I deserve to be punished. I'll pay them back if it takes the rest of my life," sobbed Cassie.

"It's my fault too," admitted Caleb. "I knew better. I'll do whatever you tell me so I can earn the money to help Cassie pay."

"Wait a minute." Their dad put up his hands. "What's going on?"

Caleb told him the whole horrible story. Their dad said, "Kids, this is serious. Wait outside and let your mom and me talk."

Cassie and Caleb sat on the back steps. "What do you think will happen to us?" asked Cassie.

"We'll probably have to do extra chores every Saturday for ten years to make enough money to pay this debt," replied Caleb.

After a few moments Cassie said, "I guess we'll have to stop playing soccer since we'll have to work on Saturdays."

"Cassie," said Caleb, "we'll probably have to stop living!"

Finally their dad told them to come inside. "Kids, I called the Nelsons and told them what happened. They were very kind. They said not to worry about it, but of course we must replace the birdhouse. I will order another one from Germany. The birdhouse is very expensive. You could never earn enough money to pay for it. Your mom and I are going to pay this debt for you."

"You mean, we don't have to work to earn the money?" asked Caleb.

"That's right," said their dad.

"But what is our punishment?" asked Cassie hesitantly.

"There is no punishment."

"Why?" asked Caleb solemnly.

"Because we love you and you belong to us," said their dad.

Cassie and Caleb ran to their mom and dad and hugged them. "Thank you, thank you," they said over and over.

"Now, kids, let's talk," said their dad. "You stood before us guilty of a debt so big you could not possibly pay it. Your mom and I thought about how we stand before God guilty of a debt we cannot possibly pay. But Jesus said, 'I will pay their debt for them. I will take the punishment for their sin.' Then Jesus did something else. He gave us His righteousness."

Their mom said, "We are going to take some splinters from that birdhouse and put them in a box for each of you. Whenever you look at those splinters, we want you to think about Jesus who died on the cross to pay the debt for your sins. We want you to think about how God the Father declared you to be justified, made righteous, because of what Jesus did for you. Why did He do it? Because He loves you and you belong to Him. Our prayer is that you will always show your gratitude to Him by loving Him and doing what He commands."

Let's Talk

1. What happened in this story?

2. Why did Cassie and Caleb's parents pay the children's debt?

3. Who paid our sin debt?

4. What does Jesus give to us?

Let's Pray

God made him who had no sin to be sin for us, so that in him we might become the righteousness of God.
(2 CORINTHIANS 5:21)

Thank God that Jesus took your sin and gives you His righteousness. Ask Him for grace to glorify Him in all you do.

Q. How can God justify you?

A. By forgiving all my sins and declaring me to be righteous.

Mimi's Bell

Cassie was going to spend the night with her grandmother. It was always fun at Mimi's house, and this time it would be doubly fun because her friend Mary Kate was going with her. Mimi promised that they could dress up in some of her old clothes, and they would have a fancy tea party.

When Cassie and Mary Kate arrived, Mimi took them to the wonderful room where they would sleep in the big four-poster bed. On the bed were some hats, gloves, fancy dresses, ribbons, and pretty scarves. "Now, girls," said Mimi, "get dressed up, and when you hear me ring my little china bell, come to the dining room for tea."

Cassie and Mary Kate giggled as they each put on one of Mimi's old dresses. They draped scarves and ribbons around themselves. They each selected a hat and laughed out loud as the feathers on the hats tickled their faces. When they heard the tinkling of the bell, each slipped her hands into a pair of Mimi's white gloves. They were quite a sight when they strolled into the dining room.

"Oh, how beautiful!" exclaimed Mary Kate as she looked at the silver teapot and the little china cups. When the girls were seated, Cassie's grandmother carefully put the little bell in the china cabinet, poured pink lemonade into their cups, and served dainty sandwiches and cake. Cassie looked at the beautiful little bell and said, "Mimi, tell us the story about your little bell."

Mimi smiled. "This bell belonged to my mother. Her daddy gave it to her for her tenth birthday. When I was a little girl, she always rang this bell when it was time for a meal. I loved the sound, and when I got married, she gave it to me. My mother was a very special lady who

prayed for me and taught me about Jesus. This bell brings back sweet memories of her."

After a delightful tea party, Cassie and Mary Kate paraded around the house in their finery and then put their jeans back on and went outside to play. That night Mimi read stories to the girls. Then they all knelt beside the big bed and prayed, and Mimi kissed them good night.

Cassie and Mary Kate woke up early the next morning. "Let's go to the kitchen and get some milk," suggested Cassie. When they passed the dining room, Cassie whispered, "Let's look at the pretty things in Mimi's china cabinet." Then Cassie did something she should never have done. She opened the china cabinet and picked up the little china bell. But somehow it slipped through her fingers and dropped to the floor. It broke into several pieces. Cassie and Mary Kate were horrified.

"Oh no," sobbed Cassie. "I knew the rule about opening Mimi's china cabinet. I broke the rule, and now look what happened. What can I do? How can I tell Mimi? She's going to hate me."

Cassie put her face in her hands and wept while Mary Kate watched in dismay. Then the girls heard Mimi's gentle voice. "Oh, Cassie, I could never hate you. I love you."

Cassie ran into Mimi's open arms. "I'm sorry, Mimi. I'm so sorry. What can I do to pay you back?"

Mimi held Cassie close as she said, "Cassie, you can't pay me back, but I forgive you anyway. And I want to do more than forgive you. I want to give you a gift." Mimi went to the china cabinet, reached to the top shelf, and picked up a beautiful glass bell. "This is the bell my mother gave me for my sixteenth birthday. It is a very expensive crystal bell. I want you to have it. We can keep it here on this shelf until you are older, but I want you to know that it is yours."

"Do you mean you forgive me for breaking your bell *and* you give me a gift of another bell? Why would you do that, Mimi?" asked Cassie.

"Because I want you girls to remember something very important," replied Mimi. "We all break God's commandments, but He forgives us. He also gives us a very expensive gift. He gives us the righteousness of Jesus. I hope this little bell will be a reminder to you of God's amazing grace."

Let's Talk

1. What happened in this story?
2. What did Mimi do when Cassie broke the bell?
3. What did Mimi want Cassie and Mary Kate to remember?

Let's Pray

God made him who had no sin to be sin for us, so that in him we might become the righteousness of God.

(2 CORINTHIANS 5:21)

Thank God that Jesus took your sin and gives you His righteousness. Ask Him for grace to glorify Him in all you do.

Q. How can God sanctify you?

A. By making me holy in heart and conduct.

Q. What must you do to be saved?

A. I must repent of my sins, believe in Christ, and live a new life.

Q. How do you repent of your sins?

A. By being sorry enough for my sin to hate and forsake it.

Q. Why must you hate and forsake your sin?

A. Because it displeases God.

Sad About Sin

Every Saturday afternoon Caleb, Angus, and Daniel meet in Caleb's tent for Truth Time. They tell each other whether or not they read their Bibles every day, and they say the memory verse for Sunday school.

"I sure am glad we have Truth Time," said Caleb one Saturday. "Several days this week I didn't want to read my Bible, but I remembered that I would have to tell you guys the truth, so I did it. Afterwards I was glad I did."

Caleb and Angus noticed that Daniel was very quiet. He looked sad. "Hey, Dan, are you okay?" asked Caleb.

"Well, I guess I'd better tell you the truth. I doubt that you'll still want to be my friends," said Daniel.

"Sure we will," said Angus.

"Well," said Daniel slowly, "I don't think that I'm a Christian."

"Sure you are, Daniel," said Caleb. "I remember when you asked Jesus to be your Savior. Why don't you think you are a Christian?"

"Because I'm so bad," moaned Daniel. "I just keep thinking and saying and doing sinful things. I didn't read my Bible a single time this week. I lied to my mom when she asked if I did my chores, and I got so angry when our soccer team lost that I was not a good sport."

Caleb and Angus thought for a few minutes. Then Angus said, "You know, Daniel, I'm just as bad as you are—probably worse. But don't you remember what we've been

learning? We're not saved by being good. We're saved by God's grace. None of us deserves to be saved. We deserve God's wrath and curse, but He gives us His love."

Just then Caleb's dad popped his head into the tent. "Hi, Truth Team, what's up?" he asked.

"Hey, Dad," Caleb greeted him. "Good timing. We've got another question for you."

The boys told Caleb's dad about their discussion. Then Dad said, "Actually, Daniel, the fact that you are so aware of your sinfulness and so bothered by it is a sign that you *are* a Christian. When you were spiritually dead in your sins, you were not bothered by your sin. But now the Holy Spirit has given you a new heart that loves God, so you are bothered when you do something that displeases Him. But here's the good part. Boys, turn in your Bibles to I John 1:8-9. As we read this, remember that this is written to Christians."

"I've got it," said Angus. Then he read: "'If we claim to be without sin, we deceive ourselves and the truth is not in us. If we confess our sins, he is faithful and just and will forgive us our sins and purify us from all unrighteousness.'"

"You see, guys," said Caleb's dad, "the Holy Spirit lets our conscience know when we sin and makes us sorry for it. He gives us grace to repent and to confess our sins to God. Then our heavenly Father forgives and cleanses us. This is part of our sanctification. That's a big word, but it just means that God makes us holy in our hearts and in our behavior. The old Puritans used to pray for the gift of tears. They wanted God to make them weep over their sin, not so they would be sad, but so they would go to God for forgiveness. Then God turns our weeping into gladness."

"Wow, Daniel," said Caleb, "your sadness over your sin shows that God is sanctifying you. I think I need to pray that I will be more sad about *my* sin."

Let's Talk

1. Why did Daniel think that Caleb and Angus would not want to be his friends?

2. Are we saved by being good?

3. Why should we hate and forsake our sin?

4. When we repent of our sin, what does God do?

5. Who makes us sorry for our sin and then gives us grace to repent?

Let's Pray

Search me, O God, and know my heart; test me and know my anxious thoughts. See if there is any offensive way in me, and lead me in the way everlasting. (PSALM 139:23-24)

Make these words your prayer.

Q. What does it mean to believe in Christ?

A. To trust in Him alone for my salvation.

Q. Can you repent and believe by your own power?

A. No—I cannot do anything good unless the Holy Spirit enables me.

Q. How can you get the help of the Holy Spirit?

A. God will give the Holy Spirit to those who ask Him.

I Did It!

Cassie and Caleb have been crossing off days on the calendar. The day finally arrived for their family to leave on a camping trip. The children put their sleeping bags and back-packs in the van, their dad prayed for traveling mercies, and they were off.

"I can't wait until we get to the campground," said Caleb. "I want to sign up with the park ranger to take one of the nature hikes."

"I want to swim in the pool," said Cassie. "And this year I want to learn to jump off the diving board."

They all laughed as they remembered Caleb's diving experience last year. "I think I walked to the edge of the diving board fifty times before I got the nerve to jump," said Caleb. "But don't worry, Cassie. I can do it now, and I'll help you."

They arrived at the park and got settled at their campsite. "Get your swimsuits on, kids, and we'll go to the pool," said their dad.

As they walked to the pool, Cassie kept saying, "I'm going to do it. I'm going to do it." When they got there, she headed straight for the diving board. Without a moment's hesitation she walked to the end of the board. Then she froze.

"Come on, Cassie. You can do it!" shouted Caleb. After what seemed like hours, Cassie turned and walked away. Caleb was waiting for her. "That's okay, Cassie. It took me a long time last year. I have an idea. I'll walk to the end of the diving board with you. We'll hold hands and jump off together."

Cassie's face brightened. "Thanks, Caleb. I can do it if we do it together."

The two of them walked to the end of the diving board. Caleb took Cassie's hand and said, "I'll count to three, and we'll jump. One, two, THREE!"

Caleb jumped. Cassie jerked her hand out of his and was left standing on the diving board. When Caleb's head popped up from the water, he looked at Cassie in astonishment. But he quickly remembered his big brother responsibility and said, "It's okay, Cassie. I have another idea. You jump and I'll catch you."

Cassie looked down at Caleb. She knew it wasn't far to the water, but from her position perched on the end of the diving board, it may as well have been a mile. As much as she loved her brother, he just didn't seem big enough and strong enough.

"Come on, Cassie," Caleb said again as he flapped his arms in the water. "I'll catch you."

"I don't think so," said Cassie. She turned and walked away from the diving board and then plopped down between her mom and dad.

"Let's talk about this, Cassie," urged her mom. "Why are you afraid to jump?"

Cassie thought a minute and then said, "I'm afraid of what will happen when I go under the water. Will I come back up? Will I be able to swim to the side?"

"Then I have an idea," said her dad. "I'll get in the water and be there when you jump. I'll be sure you come up and that you can swim to the side."

Her dad got in the water. Cassie walked to the end of the diving board. And she jumped. "I did it!" she yelled triumphantly when she bobbed up from the water.

That night as they sat around the campfire, their mom said, "Kids, I think there is a lesson in what happened today. Do you remember our catechism question: 'What does it mean to believe in Christ?'"

"'To trust in Him alone for my salvation,'" said Cassie and Caleb together.

"Cassie, when you were trying to jump off the diving board, you were afraid to let

Caleb help you. But when your dad got in the water, you trusted him. You knew he was *able* to get you to the side of the pool. You love Caleb, and you appreciated his offer of help, but you were not willing to trust him because you were not sure he could really do what you needed him to do. You see, it is not enough for us to believe with our minds that Jesus died on the cross. We must also trust that He is able to save us and take us to heaven."

"Now," said their dad, "let's see if our catechism kids can answer this question. Cassie could jump off the diving board by herself, but can you repent of your sin and trust Jesus in your own power?"

"No," said Cassie and Caleb. "I cannot do anything good unless the Holy Spirit enables me."

"The catechism kids did it again!" laughed their dad.

Let's Talk

1. What happened in the story?
2. Why wouldn't Cassie jump off the diving board when Caleb offered to catch her?
3. Can we in our own power trust Jesus to be our Savior?

Let's Pray

I will give you a new heart and put a new spirit in you; I will remove from you your heart of stone and give you a heart of flesh. And I will put my Spirit in you and move you to follow my decrees and be careful to keep my laws. (Ezekiel 36:26-27)

Thank God that His Holy Spirit gives us a new heart so that we can trust in Christ. Ask God for grace to glorify Him in all you think and do and say.

Q. How long ago did Christ die?

A. About two thousand years.

Q. How were sinners saved before Christ came?

A. By believing in a Messiah to come.

Q. How did they show their faith?

A. By offering the sacrifices God required.

Q. What did these sacrifices represent?

A. Christ, the Lamb of God, who would come to die for sinners.

The Hike

Cassie and Caleb were having a great time on the camping trip. Every day they had a new adventure. Every night they read stories and played games with their mom and dad.

One night after they read a Bible story, their dad explained how the Bible is divided into the Old Testament and the New Testament. He told them that the Old Testament was written before Jesus came.

Suddenly a new thought came to Cassie. "Dad," she asked, "how were people saved before Jesus came and died on the cross?"

"Good question, Cassie," said her dad. "When Adam and Eve sinned, God promised that He would send a *Messiah*. Messiah means Savior. Before Jesus came, people were saved by believing God's promise. So people have always been saved by believing in Jesus—either that He was *going* to come or that He *has* come." Then their dad prayed that God would use their family to help other people know about Jesus and that Cassie and Caleb would always glorify God.

As everyone crawled into a sleeping bag, Caleb said, "I can hardly wait until tomorrow." The whole family knew why he was so excited. This was the first year he was old enough to go on the all-day nature hike with the park ranger.

Early the next morning, Caleb's dad took him to the place where the hike was to begin. "Have a good time, son, and remember that everything you will see was created by our sovereign God. Psalm 19:1 says: 'The heavens declare the glory of God; the skies proclaim

the work of his hands.' Enjoy His creation and praise Him for all you see."

The park ranger introduced himself as Ranger Sam. He asked each of the boys and girls to introduce themselves. Then he paired them up so everyone would have a buddy. Caleb was paired with a boy named Scotty.

As they walked along, Caleb and Scotty discovered that they were both on a soccer team and that they both liked to read about dinosaurs. "This is so cool," said Caleb. "I'm glad we're buddies."

On their first stop, Ranger Sam talked about some of the rock formations and about

the various kinds of trees.

When they started walking again, Caleb said, "When you look at all of the different kinds of rocks and trees, doesn't it make you think about how great and powerful God is to have created so many different things?"

"What do you mean?" asked Scotty. "I never thought about God creating things. I guess I never think about God at all."

Caleb didn't know what to say. Then he remembered that every day his mom and dad prayed that God would use their family to help other people know about Jesus. Caleb said a prayer in his heart and asked the Holy Spirit to help him know what to say.

"The Bible says that God made everything. He made us, and He wants us to live with Him in heaven. But we can't go to heaven unless our sins are forgiven. Jesus came into the world to die for our sins."

"You sure are religious," Scotty scoffed. "I don't believe all that stuff."

Caleb started to argue with Scotty, but then he remembered that no one *can* repent and believe without the help of the Holy Spirit. *I guess I should just pray for Scotty*, thought Caleb to himself.

When they stopped for lunch, Scotty sat with some other boys, and Caleb heard him say, "That guy Caleb is too religious for me."

Caleb felt very alone, but as he was getting his lunch out of his backpack, someone said, "Hi, Caleb. May I sit with you?"

Caleb looked up. It was Ranger Sam. "Sure," said Caleb.

Then Ranger Sam asked, "Would you like to thank the Lord for our food?"

"Sure," said Caleb again.

B I G   T R U T H S

After they prayed, Ranger Sam said, "Caleb, I overheard your conversation with Scotty. I'm a Christian, and I was blessed by your courage to witness for Jesus. I want to live for God's glory, but too often I'm afraid to talk to others about my faith, but you have encouraged me to tell others about our Savior."

"But what good did it do?" asked Caleb. "Now Scotty doesn't like me, and he still doesn't believe in Jesus."

"Well, Caleb, it did a lot of good. First, you obeyed God, and that's what is important. Second, you planted a seed of truth in Scotty's mind. Now we must pray for the Holy Spirit to keep reminding Scotty about what you said and to cause him to repent of his sin and trust Jesus. Why don't we become prayer partners and pray for Scotty?"

Caleb and Ranger Sam gave each other a high five as they said together, "Partners!"

Let's Talk

1. How were people saved before Jesus came and died on the cross?

2. What does the word *Messiah* mean?

3. What happened in the story?

Let's Pray

Trust in the LORD with all your heart and lean not on your own understanding; in all your ways acknowledge him, and he will make your paths straight. Do not be wise in your own eyes; fear the LORD and shun evil. (PROVERBS 3:5-7)

Ask God for grace to do what these verses teach us.

17

Q. How many offices did the Lord Jesus fulfill as the promised Messiah?

A. He fulfilled three offices.

Q. What are they?

A. The offices of prophet, priest, and king.

Q. How is Christ your prophet?

A. He teaches me the will of God.

Q. How is Christ your priest?

A. He died for my sins and prays for me.

Q. How is Christ your king?

A. He rules over me and defends me.

Spiritual Eyes

The all-day nature hike was better than Caleb had thought it would be. "We had the greatest time," he told his mom, dad, and Cassie. "Ranger Sam is really cool. He's a Christian, and we're going to be prayer partners and pray for Scotty because he doesn't believe in Jesus."

"We'll pray for Scotty too," said Cassie.

The next day at the playground, Caleb saw Scotty and some other boys. "Hi, Scotty," said Caleb.

Caleb heard Scotty say to the other boys, "Here comes that weird guy I told you about." Then Scotty said in a mocking voice, "Hi, Caleb. Do you want to go with us? We're going to the camp store and steal some candy."

"You're going to do what?" asked an astonished Caleb. "It's wrong to steal."

"See," said Scotty to the other boys. "I told you he's weird."

Caleb turned and ran back to his campsite. As soon as his dad saw him, he asked, "Caleb, what's wrong? You look pretty shook up."

Caleb told his dad what had happened. "Wow," said his dad. "I see why you were frightened. Son, I'm proud of you for running away from sin."

"Dad, am I weird?" asked Caleb.

"No, Caleb. But you need to understand that as Christians, we belong to God's kingdom. People who are not Christians will often think we are strange. They don't understand why we don't do the things they do. They see the world and themselves differently

than we do. Think about it this way, Caleb. When you look through your microscope, you see things that you can't see with your eyes alone. When we become Christians, God opens our spiritual eyes so that we can know and understand things we can't know and understand without His power. We see God as the sovereign Creator and King over the universe. We understand that we are sinners and that Jesus is our prophet who teaches us, our priest who died for us, and our king who rules and defends us. We know that our purpose is to glorify God. Listen to these verses from I Peter 2:9-12:

"'But you are a chosen people, a royal priesthood, a holy nation, a people belonging to God, that you may declare the praises of him who called you out of darkness into his wonderful light. Once you were not a people, but

now you are the people of God; once you had not received mercy, but now you have received mercy. Dear friends, I urge you, as aliens and strangers in the world, to abstain from sinful desires, which war against your soul. Live such good lives among the pagans that, though they accuse you of doing wrong, they may see your good deeds and glorify God on the day he visits us.'

"Caleb," continued his dad, "we see the world as God's creation and ourselves as His children. People who are not Christians will sometimes think we are weird, but we must love them and live a good and holy life before them so they will see our good deeds and glorify God."

"I'm glad I'm a child of the King," said Caleb. "Dad, can we pray that Scotty will see the world and himself with spiritual eyes?"

"Sure, son," replied his dad.

Let's Talk

1. What did you learn from this story?
2. What kingdom do Christians belong to?
3. How does it make you feel to know that God rules and defends you?

Let's Pray

Trust in the LORD with all your heart and lean not on your own understanding; in all your ways acknowledge him, and he will make your paths straight. Do not be wise in your own eyes; fear the LORD and shun evil. (PROVERBS 3:5-7)

Ask God for grace to do what these verses teach us.

Q. Why do you need Christ as your prophet?

A. Because I am ignorant by nature.

Q. Why do you need Christ as your priest?

A. Because I am guilty of breaking God's law.

Q. Why do you need Christ as your king?

A. Because I am weak and helpless.

From Grumpy to Grateful

Cassie woke up very excited. While Caleb was on the all-day nature hike, she had practiced jumping off the diving board. She could hardly wait to show Caleb how well she could jump. She had even jumped off backward.

"Wake up, Caleb," Cassie squealed. "It's morning!"

"Leave me alone," Caleb snapped.

Cassie's feelings were hurt. She crawled out of the tent and started helping her mom prepare breakfast. When breakfast was ready, their dad asked Caleb to thank the Lord for their food. "I don't feel like praying today," Caleb sulked.

Later that afternoon, they were discussing what they would do after dinner. "Nothing sounds fun to me," Caleb mumbled.

"Caleb," said his dad, "we've noticed that you seem to be pretty grumpy today."

"Well, I feel grumpy, and I don't know what to do about it," said Caleb in a sad voice.

"I think this situation with Scotty is really bothering you," said his mom.

"It makes me mad to think about how Scotty has been treating me," Caleb quickly responded.

"Caleb," said his dad, "the Bible says that we have all sinned and come short of the glory of God. This morning you sinned when you were mean to your sister. She wanted to show you how well she can jump off the diving board, but when she tried to tell you, you snapped at her and hurt her feelings. It's not that much different from what Scotty did to you. He said some things that hurt your feelings, didn't he?"

"Oh no," said Caleb. "I've been acting like Scotty. I'll try to do better."

"I'm glad you want to do better, Caleb, but let me explain something to you," said his dad. "We *can't* do better. We are all sinful. We are ignorant of God's law, we break His law, and we are too weak to obey His law. We are no better than Scotty. But there is a huge difference between Scotty and us. We have the Lord Jesus living in our hearts. He is our prophet, our priest, and our king. He teaches us His law, He prays for us, and He gives us the power to glorify Him. We can't just try to act better. We must ask God to change us."

Caleb was quiet for a few minutes, and then he asked, "So what should I do about my grumpy attitude?"

"Well, Caleb, I think we need to start by thanking God that He loves us. Let's thank Him that He is our prophet, priest, and king. Let's ask Him for grace to love Him and to obey Him."

That is exactly what they did. And as Caleb thought about God's love rather than about Scotty's meanness, his grumpiness slowly changed to gratefulness.

Let's Talk

1. Why was Caleb in a grumpy mood?
2. How had Caleb acted like Scotty?
3. When Caleb said he would try to act better, what did his dad tell him?
4. When Caleb asked what he should do about his grumpy attitude, what did his dad tell him?

Let's Pray

Trust in the LORD with all your heart and lean not on your own understanding; in all your ways acknowledge him, and he will make your paths straight. Do not be wise in your own eyes; fear the LORD and shun evil. (PROVERBS 3:5-7)

Ask God for grace to do what these verses teach us.

Q. How many commandments did God write down on the stone tablets?

A. Ten commandments.

Q. What do the first four commandments teach you?

A. What it means to love and serve God.

Q. What do the last six commandments teach you?

A. What it means to love and serve my neighbor.

Q. What is the sum of the Ten Commandments?

A. To love God with all my heart, and my neighbor as myself.

Q. Who is your neighbor?

A. Everybody is my neighbor.

Q. Is God pleased if you love and obey Him?

A. Yes. He loves those who love Him.

Q. Is God displeased with those who refuse to love and obey Him?

A. Yes. God is angry with the wicked every day.

New Buddies!

Cassie and Caleb were up early. It was the last day of their camping trip, and they didn't want to miss a minute. After breakfast their dad opened his Bible and read 2 Chronicles 6:14: "O LORD, God of Israel, there is no God like you in heaven or on earth—you who keep your covenant of love with your servants who continue wholeheartedly in your way."

Their dad continued, "Now let's say the verse we have been memorizing." The family recited 2 Chronicles 15:12: "'They entered into a covenant to seek the LORD, the God of their fathers, with all their heart and soul.'"

"God is always faithful to His covenant promise," said their dad, " but for us to enjoy His covenant blessings, we must love and serve Him wholeheartedly. He gave us His commandments to help us know how to love and serve Him, and He gives us his Holy Spirit to give us power to love and serve Him. Caleb, when Scotty tried to get you to disobey the eighth commandment that says, 'You shall not steal,' it was God's grace that gave you the power to run away from that temptation. When you did that, you loved and served God. Every day there will be temptations to disobey God, but we must enter into a covenant with one another to seek the Lord and to live by His commandments."

Later at the pool Caleb saw Scotty. "Hi, Scotty," he said.

"I'm surprised you still want to talk to me," remarked Scotty.

"Sure I want to talk to you," Caleb told him.

"Look, Caleb, I don't know what happened to me the other day. When we got to the camp store, I felt awful about stealing. I've stolen things before, and it never bothered me, but I kept thinking about you saying it was wrong. Suddenly I was scared. You're different, but I'm not so sure you're weird. Maybe I'm the one who's weird."

"I don't know if we're weird," said Caleb, "but I do know we're all sinners, and we need a Savior."

"But I'm not good enough to be a Christian," said Scotty. "You don't know all the bad things I've done."

"None of us can be good enough," said Caleb. "We would have to be perfect, and no one is perfect except Jesus. He kept God's law and died to pay for our sins."

"Why would He do that?" asked Scotty.

"Because He loves us," Caleb answered.

"But if I become a Christian, I can't be like you. I can't be that good," admitted Scotty.

"Look, Scotty, when Jesus comes into your heart, He gives you His Holy Spirit to help you. We still sin, but He helps us to love and serve Him," explained Caleb.

"What do I have to do?" asked Scotty.

Just at that moment Ranger Sam walked up. "Hi, guys, what's up?"

Caleb gave him a big grin. "You're just in time, prayer partner. Scotty wants to ask Jesus to be his Savior."

"Wow," said Ranger Sam. The three of them bowed their heads.

"What do I say?" asked Scotty.

"Just tell Jesus that you know you're a sinner and that you're sorry for your sin. Ask

Him to be your Savior," said Ranger Sam.

Scotty prayed, and then Caleb thanked the Lord for saving Scotty. Ranger Sam prayed that Scotty would grow in the grace and the knowledge of his Savior.

"Oh man, this is great!" said Caleb. "I have an idea. Second Chronicles 15:12 says, 'They entered into a covenant to seek the LORD, the God of their fathers, with all their heart and soul.' Why don't we enter into a covenant to be E-mail buddies and to help each other seek the Lord with all our heart and soul?"

The three of them gave high fives as they said, "Buddies!"

Let's Talk

1. Why did Scotty think he couldn't be a Christian?

2. Can we be good enough to be Christians?

3. Who kept God's law for us?

4. What did you like about this story?

Let's Pray

"Teacher, which is the greatest commandment in the Law?" Jesus replied: "'Love the Lord your God with all your heart and with all your soul and with all your mind.' This is the first and greatest commandment. And the second is like it: 'Love your neighbor as yourself.'" (MATTHEW 22:36-39)

Ask God for grace to do what Jesus teaches us in these verses.

Q. What is the first commandment?

A. "You shall have no other gods before me"
(Exodus 20:2).

Q. What does the first commandment teach you?

A. To worship the true God and Him alone.

A Bad Decision

Dad, can we please go on the afternoon hike with Ranger Sam?" begged Cassie and Caleb. "We want to tell everyone good-by before we go home."

"We really need to get on the road," said their dad. "But I know you want to see all your friends. It will make us very late getting home, but I guess we'll stay."

It was even later than they expected when they arrived at home, and everyone went straight to bed. Sunday morning they slept later than usual. Everything was disorganized, and the whole family ran around like crazy trying to find clean clothes and eat a quick bowl of cereal so they could make it to church on time.

"Hurry, Cassie. You can put your shoes on in the car," called her mother.

"I can't find my Bible. Mom, *where* is my Bible?" grumbled Caleb.

"Come on, everyone—we're going to be late," snapped their dad.

"Hi, guys," called Daniel as he ran across the yard and jumped into the car. "I sure missed you while you were on your camping trip. Was it fun?"

There was silence. "Didn't you have a good time?" asked Daniel.

"We did have a good time, Daniel. I guess we're all a little rattled this morning," replied Mom.

"Oh no!" wailed Cassie. "I forgot my offering. And I don't know my memory verse."

"Just ignore her," said Caleb, and he began telling Daniel about their trip.

Cassie pouted all the way to church, but when she got to her Sunday school class, she started telling everyone about their trip. Her Sunday school teacher even had to move her to a different table so she would stop talking to her friends. Caleb hardly listened at all in church because he was too busy sending notes to Angus about his camping adventures. They all got tickled during church because their dad kept dozing.

On the way home from church Cassie said, "What's for lunch, Mom?"

"What's for lunch?!" her mother snapped. "We didn't get home until late last night. I have piles of dirty laundry to do. I have not even thought about lunch. The only thing I can think about right now is a nap."

"But, Mom, I'm hungry," whined Cassie.

Daniel was very quiet. Then he whispered to Caleb, "I've never seen your family like this. Are you sure you had a good time on your vacation?"

Caleb's dad heard Daniel, and suddenly he realized that his family had not worshiped God that day. They had been at church, but they had not worshiped. He prayed silently and asked the Lord for forgiveness. He asked for wisdom to talk with his family. He pulled the car into the driveway, turned off the motor, and said, "I need to ask all of you to forgive me."

"For what?" asked everyone at once.

"I made a bad decision yesterday," said their dad. "We all wanted to stay at the campground a little longer, but I should have realized that it was not a good idea. What do we usually do on Saturday night?"

"Mom helps us get our clothes and Bibles and offering together so everything will be ready on Sunday morning," said Cassie.

"You help us with our memory verses and catechism," said Caleb.

"And what do we do on Sunday morning?" asked their dad.

"We all eat breakfast together, and you read the Bible to us," said Cassie.

"And on the way to church you talk to us and tell us that worship means that we praise God because He is worthy to be praised," said Caleb.

"You always tell us that worshiping God is the most important thing we do and that we should be very serious about it," added Daniel.

"When we get to church, you or mom pray that we

will worship God in a way that will glorify Him," put in Cassie.

Their dad said, "Kids, I allowed our family to do something that kept us from worshiping the Lord as we should. I certainly didn't glorify God when I dozed during the sermon. We were tired and grumpy and unprepared. I asked the Lord to forgive me, and now I ask you to forgive me."

There were lots of hugs, everyone helped mom make peanut butter and jelly sandwiches, and they all took a nap so they would be rested before they went to church Sunday night.

Let's Talk

1. What difference did it make when Cassie and Caleb's family did not prepare for worship?
2. What does it mean to worship God?
3. What is the most important thing we do?
4. Do we glorify God if we go to church but do not really worship Him?

Let's Pray

"Teacher, which is the greatest commandment in the Law?" Jesus replied: "'Love the Lord your God with all your heart and with all your soul and with all your mind.' This is the first and greatest commandment. And the second is like it: 'Love your neighbor as yourself.'" (MATTHEW 22:36-39)

Ask God for grace to obey the first commandment.

Q. What is the second commandment?

A. "You shall not make for yourself a carved image—any likeness of anything that is in heaven above, or that is in the earth beneath, or that is in the water under the earth; you shall not bow down to them nor serve them. For I, the LORD your God, am a jealous God, visiting the iniquity of the fathers upon the children to the third and fourth generations of those who hate Me, but showing mercy to thousands, to those who love Me and keep My commandments" (Exodus 20:4 nkjv).

Q. What does the second commandment teach you?

A. To worship God in a proper manner and to avoid idolatry. (original edition)

Cassie Wants a New Doll

Cassie and Caleb got an allowance of one dollar every week. Their mom gave them two quarters, four dimes, and two nickels. They each have three boxes. Box #1 has "Tithe" written on it. Box #2 says "Savings." Box #3 says "Spending." They each put a dime in the Tithe box because the Bible teaches that we should give a tenth of all we have to the Lord. Then the children could decide how much they wanted to save, but the rule was that they must save something each week.

One day after visiting Mary Kate, Cassie said, "Mom, you should see Mary Kate's new doll. It is so beautiful. Mary Kate and her doll have dresses just alike. May I get a doll like that and get a dress to match?"

Her mom replied, "Those dolls are beautiful, but they are expensive. I have an idea. Your birthday is in eight weeks. You save half the money, and we'll give you the other half for your birthday. I'll give you extra chores to earn some money."

"Good deal," said Cassie. "Will you give me some chores now?"

"Sure," said her mom. "I'll pay you at the end of the week when you get your allowance, but you can't neglect your regular chores."

That week Cassie earned five dollars. She decided to save *all* of her allowance. That would mean she would have *six* dollars. She really wanted that doll.

When her mom gave her the money, there were five one-dollar bills, two quarters, four dimes, and two nickels. Then Cassie remembered that she was to put money in the Tithe box.

"Mom, how much do I tithe for the five dollars I earned?" she asked.

"A tenth of five dollars is fifty cents," said her mom.

"Do you mean I have to put fifty cents plus the dime for my allowance in the Tithe box?" asked Cassie.

"Well, Cassie, the Bible teaches us to give a tithe to the Lord, but it also says that God loves a cheerful giver. Maybe you need to ask Him to give you grace to *want* to give to Him."

"Okay," said Cassie as she reluctantly put sixty cents in the Tithe box and all the rest in the Savings box.

Then Cassie's mom said, "Cassie, you did such a good job that I am going to give you this list of chores. If you have them all done by next Saturday, I'll pay you ten dollars."

"Ten dollars!" exclaimed Cassie. "Give me the list!"

Monday afternoon Cassie was polishing silver when her mother said, "Cassie, let's make some cookies and take them to Susie. Since she broke her leg, she can't go outside to play."

"I can't today, Mom," said Cassie. "I want to get some chores done."

Wednesday Cassie's mom said, "Cassie, let's write a note to Grandmom. She isn't feeling well, and a note from you would cheer her."

"Later, Mom. I want to get some chores done," said Cassie.

Friday Cassie's mom said, "Cassie, I'm going to call Grandmom and check on her. Do you want to talk to her?"

"Not today, Mom," said Cassie. "I've got too much to do."

Saturday morning Cassie finished the chores. Her mom gave her one five-dollar bill, five one-dollar bills, two quarters, four dimes, and two nickels.

"How much is a tithe of ten dollars?" asked Cassie.

"One dollar," said her mom.

Once again Cassie reluctantly put one dollar and one dime in her Tithe box. Then she put all the rest in her Savings box.

Saturday night Cassie's mom said, "Okay, kids, let's review the catechism. Caleb, what is the second commandment?" After Caleb recited the answer, their mom asked Cassie, "What does the second commandment teach you?"

"Well," said Cassie slowly, "I've been so busy earning money for the doll that I didn't study my catechism."

"I can say it," said Caleb. "'To worship God in a proper manner and to avoid idolatry.'"

"Mom," asked Cassie, "has the doll that I want become an idol to me?"

"Cassie," replied her mom, "I've been praying that you would think about that. There's nothing wrong with wanting the doll. And there's certainly nothing wrong with working hard to earn the money. But we must be careful that we don't let other things become so important that we love them more than we love God and His people. Let's thank the Lord for helping you realize that you let something else have first place in your life, and let's ask Him to help us both love Him with all our hearts and love others as we love ourselves."

Let's Talk

1. How was the allowance money to be divided?

2. How did Cassie let the doll become an idol?

3. What are some other things that can become idols in our lives?

Let's Pray

"Teacher, which is the greatest commandment in the Law?" Jesus replied: "'Love the Lord your God with all your heart and with all your soul and with all your mind.' This is the first and greatest commandment. And the second is like it: 'Love your neighbor as yourself.'" (MATTHEW 22:36-39)

Ask God for grace to obey the second commandment.

Q. What is the third commandment?

A. "You shall not take the name of the LORD your God in vain, for the LORD will not hold Him guiltless who takes His name in vain" (Exodus 20:7 nkjv).

Q. What does the third commandment teach you?

A. To reverence God's name, word, and works. (original edition)

Q. What is the third commandment?

A. "You shall not take the name of the LORD your God in vain, for the LORD will not hold Him guiltless who takes His name in vain" (Exodus 20:7 nkjv).

Q. What does the third commandment teach you?

A. To reverence God's name, word, and works. (original edition)

Daniel's Prayer Request

Truth Time," Caleb, Angus, and Daniel said as they gave each other high fives. Then the boys went into Caleb's tent.

"Okay, guys," said Caleb. "I have to 'fess up. Three days this week I did not read my Bible. There is no excuse. I just got lazy. The bad thing is that when I skipped Monday, it was a lot easier to skip Tuesday, and then I totally forgot on Wednesday. Thursday I was kicking the soccer ball with Cassie, and I looked over and noticed this tent. Suddenly I remembered that I would have to sit in here and face you guys today. Then when I started memorizing our verse for this week, I was really bummed."

"I don't get it," said Daniel. "What did this verse have to do with you reading the Bible? Exodus 20:7 says, 'You shall not take the name of the LORD your God in vain; for the LORD will not hold him guiltless who takes His name in vain.'"

"Well, the catechism says that this means we are to reverence God's name, word, and works. So it is not just about saying God's name in a wrong way. I did not honor Him when I was too lazy to read His Word."

"Oh, I get it," said Daniel.

"Okay," said Angus. "Now that we have that settled, do either of you have a prayer request?"

"I do," Daniel replied. "My mom and dad swear using God's name all the time. It really makes me feel yucky. I don't know what to do."

"Wow," said Caleb. "That's tough. Do you remember our Sunday school lesson a cou-

ple of weeks ago about praying for wisdom and grace? This seems to be one of those times when we have to ask the Lord to give you wisdom to know what to do and grace to do it in a loving way."

The boys prayed that God would give Daniel wisdom and grace to know what to do when his parents used God's name in vain. During dinner one night it happened. Daniel's mom spilled some coffee, and she swore using God's name.

Without thinking, Daniel jumped up and got a towel for his mom. Then it was almost as if he heard words coming from his mouth that he had not thought about. "Mom," he said softly, "could I ask you a favor? It makes me sad when you and Dad use God's name in vain. I love you, and I love God. I would feel sad and mad if someone said *your* name in a disrespectful way."

No one said anything for what seemed like a long time to Daniel. Then his mom spoke. "God is really important to you, isn't He? We've seen you change. You are kinder and more obedient and responsible. Are you just trying harder to be good because those people at church tell you to act this way?"

Now Daniel was quiet for a minute. Finally he said, "It's not that I'm trying harder. I love God more and more, and I want to be like Him. I've learned that it is God's grace in me that makes me *want* to be different. I don't really understand it all, but since Jesus became my Savior, the Holy Spirit lives in me and helps me live for His glory."

"Maybe there's something to this church stuff," said Daniel's dad.

"I don't understand what you're talking about," said Daniel's mom, "but I'll try not to say God's name that way since it bothers you."

In his heart Daniel thanked God for giving him wisdom to know what to say and grace to say it in a loving way.

Let's Talk

1. What happened in this story?

2. What did you learn from this story?

3. How do you feel when people use God's name in vain?

4. What are some ways Daniel glorified God?

Let's Pray

"Teacher, which is the greatest commandment in the Law?" Jesus replied: "'Love the Lord your God with all your heart and with all your soul and with all your mind.' This is the first and greatest commandment. And the second is like it: 'Love your neighbor as yourself.'" (MATTHEW 22:36-39)

Ask God for grace to obey the third commandment.

Q. What is the fourth commandment?

A. "Remember the Sabbath day by keeping it holy. Six days you shall labor and do all your work, but the seventh day is a Sabbath to the LORD your God. On it you shall not do any work, neither you, nor your son or daughter, nor your manservant or maidservant, nor your animals, nor the alien within your gates. For in six days the LORD made the heavens and the earth, the sea, and all that is in them, but he rested on the seventh day. Therefore the LORD blessed the Sabbath day and made it holy" (Exodus 20:8-11).

Q. What does the fourth commandment teach you?

A. To work six days and to keep a holy Sabbath.

Q. What day of the week is the Christian Sabbath?

A. The first day of the week, which is the Lord's Day.

Q. Why is it called the Lord's Day?

A. Because on that day our Lord rose from the dead.

Q. How should you keep the Lord's Day?

A. I should rest from my daily work and faithfully worship God.

The Football Tickets

Daniel could hardly wait until Truth Time with Caleb and Angus. He was the first one at the tent.

"Hey, guys, you're not going to believe what happened." He told them about his mother saying God's name in vain and how God gave him wisdom and grace to ask her not to use God's name that way. "And here is the best part," said Daniel. "This morning Mom and Dad told me they would like to go to church with me tomorrow."

"Wow," said Caleb and Angus at the same time. "That's really cool."

"Please pray that they will listen and that they will ask Jesus to be their Savior," requested Daniel.

"Sure," the boys said.

Then they each recited their memory verse:

"Remember the Sabbath day by keeping it holy. Six days you shall labor and do all your work, but the seventh day is a Sabbath to the LORD your God. On it you shall not do any work, neither you, nor your son or daughter, nor your manservant or maidservant, nor your animals, nor the alien within your gates. For in six days the LORD made the heavens and the earth, the sea, and all that is in them, but he rested on the seventh day. Therefore the LORD blessed the Sabbath day and made it holy (Exodus 20:8)."

Just then Daniel heard his dad calling, "Dan, come here. I've got great news!"

Daniel, Caleb, and Angus came out from the tent to find Daniel's dad quite excited. "My boss just called and gave me six club-level tickets for tomorrow's football game! How would you guys and your dads like to go with Daniel and me? We can leave about ten in the morning, eat lunch on the way, and get there in time for the kickoff."

There was absolute silence.

"What's wrong?" asked Daniel's dad with a bewildered look.

"Dad, it would be great to go to the

football game, but tomorrow is Sunday. The Bible says that we are to honor the Sabbath day and keep it holy. I don't think it would be honoring to the Lord if we skipped church to go to a football game. I'm sorry, Dad, but thanks a lot."

Angus and Caleb thanked him. Daniel's dad just stared at them. Daniel didn't know whether he was mad or what! Then the man spoke very softly. "You people are really serious. I don't get it, but maybe church and God are more important. Daniel, your mom and I will still go to church with you tomorrow." He walked away shaking his head.

As soon as he was inside his house, Daniel, Angus, and Caleb looked at each other and gave a two-thumbs-up as they said, "YES!"

Let's Talk

1. Why is Sunday, the first day of the week, the Christian Sabbath?

2. What happened in this story?

3. What did the boys do that glorified God?

Let's Pray

"If you keep your feet from breaking the Sabbath and from doing as you please on my holy day, if you call the Sabbath a delight and the LORD's holy day honorable, and if you honor it by not going your own way and not doing as you please or speaking idle words, then you will find your joy in the LORD, and I will cause you to ride on the heights of the land and to feast on the inheritance of your father Jacob." The mouth of the LORD has spoken. (ISAIAH 58:13-14)

Ask God to give you grace to remember the Sabbath day and to keep it holy.

24

Q. What is the fifth commandment?

A. "Honor your father and your mother, so that you may live long in the land the LORD your God is giving you."

Q. What does the fifth commandment teach you?

A. To love and obey my parents and all others that God appoints to teach and govern me.

Q. What is the sixth commandment?

A. "You shall not murder."

Q. What does the sixth commandment teach you?

A. Not to take anyone's life unjustly.

Daniel's Parents Go to Church

Daniel was awake early. When he looked out his window, the sun was shining, and he could see that it was going to be a beautiful day. This day would be beautiful to Daniel even if it was gloomy and rainy. This was the day his parents had said they would go to church with him. Daniel prayed in his heart, "Dear Jesus, help Mom and Dad to learn about You and to trust You to be their Savior."

Daniel was surprised to hear noise in the kitchen. He slipped out of his bed and walked down the hall. His mom was preparing breakfast. "I thought we would all eat together so you can tell us what church is like," said his mom. As they sat around the table, Daniel told them about Sunday school and about church.

"But what if we don't know where to go or what to do?" asked his mom.

"Everyone is so nice. They'll tell you what to do. I know you'll like it," Daniel assured her. Then he added, "Mom, thanks for breakfast. You're a good mom."

When they got to church, Daniel saw Cassie and Caleb and their mom and dad standing in the parking lot. "Hi, we were waiting for

you," they said. "Come with us to our Sunday school class. Afterward we can meet the kids and sit together in church." Daniel's parents seemed relieved, and Daniel was thankful.

On the way home from church Daniel's mom said, "I've never heard these things before. I thought being a Christian meant that you start trying to be good. I thought it meant you have to keep all of the Ten Commandments. In Sunday school and in church I kept hearing that we need God's grace because we can't be good enough to go to heaven. I'm not sure I understand that. What is God's grace?"

Daniel was ready with the answer. "It's His love that we don't deserve," he said. "Let me show you a great way to remember what it means." He reached into his backpack and got a pencil and a piece of paper. He wrote the word *grace* down one side of the page. Then beside each letter he wrote these words:

God's

Riches

At

Christ's

Expense

"I think I understand," said Daniel's dad. "God gives us the gift of eternal life because Jesus paid the price for our sins. Wow! This is amazing."

They pulled into the driveway, and Daniel's dad turned the car off. Mom said, "It is amazing. Didn't we sing a hymn about that this morning?"

Then they heard Daniel's voice singing from the backseat: "'Amazing grace, how sweet the sound, that saved a wretch like me. I once was lost but now am found, was blind but now I see.'"

It was quiet for a few moments. Then Daniel heard his dad say, "Dear God, I'm a sinner, and I need Your grace. I believe that Jesus died for me. Please save me from my sin."

Daniel's mom said, "Me too, God. I want Jesus to be my Savior. And, God, thank You for our son who showed us what a difference You make in someone's life."

When Daniel opened his eyes, he looked next door and saw Caleb's family sitting in their car watching them. Daniel grinned and gave them a thumbs-up. Cassie, Caleb, and their parents jumped out of their car as Daniel and his mom and dad got out of their car. There was much rejoicing and praising the Lord in that driveway. And the Bible tells us that there is "rejoicing in heaven over one sinner who repents" (Luke 15:7).

Let's Talk

1. What are some ways Daniel honored his parents?

2. How did God use Daniel's obedience to help his parents want to learn about Jesus?

3. What is grace?

4. What are some of the riches that Jesus purchased for us?

Let's Pray

For it is by grace you have been saved, through faith—and this not from yourselves, it is the gift of God—not by works, so that no one can boast. (EPHESIANS 2:8-9)

Thank God for what these verses teach us.

Q. What is the seventh commandment?

A. "You shall not commit adultery" (Exodus 20:14).

Q. What does the seventh commandment teach you?

A. To be pure in heart, language, and conduct. (original edition)

Q. What is the eighth commandment?

A. "You shall not steal" (Exodus 20:15).

Q. What does the eighth commandment teach you?

A. Not to take anything owned by another person.

The Bicycle

Saturday afternoon is a favorite time for Cassie and Caleb. The whole family takes a bike ride together. Sometimes they ride around their neighborhood. Sometimes they ride to a park a few blocks away. And sometimes they ride to an ice cream store close by. It really doesn't matter where they go. It's fun because they do it together.

One Saturday as they were riding, it started drizzling rain. Before they could get home, the rain poured down. They got to their yard, threw down their bikes, and ran into the house just as a loud clap of thunder roared through the sky. They were out of breath, drenched, and laughing happily. "Get those wet clothes off, and we'll have some hot chocolate," said their mom.

The storm continued until after they went to bed, and no one thought about the bicycles in the yard.

The next morning when they started off to church, their dad noticed the bikes. "Everybody grab your bike, and let's put them in the garage before we leave."

"Wait a minute!" called Caleb. "Where's my bike?"

Everyone looked around in bewilderment. They finally realized that Caleb's bike had been stolen.

They all felt sad as they drove to church. "I can't believe someone would come into our yard and steal something that belongs to us," said Mom.

"Why would someone take Caleb's bike?" asked Cassie.

"It was such a cool bike," said Caleb.

"Caleb," said his dad, "I'm sad that someone stole your bike, but there's something that would make me even sadder."

"What?" asked Cassie and Caleb at the same time.

"If you were the person who stole someone else's bike."

That afternoon the family sat down to talk. "Caleb," Dad began, "we're sorry about your bike. It makes me sad to have to tell you that because of some extra expenses, we just don't have the money to buy another bike right now. I'm really sorry, son."

"That's okay, Dad," said Caleb. "I understand."

"You can ride my bike anytime you want," offered Cassie.

"Thanks, Cassie, but somehow I can't see myself on a pink bike with glittery streamers on the handlebars," said Caleb with a smile.

"I think this would be easier if you were being a brat about it," said Caleb's mom as she hugged him. "Seriously, I'm very blessed by God's grace in you."

"I have an idea," suggested Cassie. "Let's pray that the Lord will provide a bike for Caleb."

Her mom and dad looked at each other and grinned. "Why didn't we think of that?"

The family prayed, and Caleb's dad asked the Lord to give their family grace to glorify Him in everything they did. "Lord," said Caleb, "if You want me to have a bike, please provide it. If You don't, help me to glorify You anyway."

For the next several weeks the family went on hikes instead of riding bikes. Then one day Caleb's dad came home with a huge grin on his face.

"Come here, everybody," he called excitedly. "Today an older man at work asked me if I know anyone who needs a bicycle. He said he got one for his grandson to ride when he visits them, but the grandson is older now and doesn't ride the bike anymore. He said it's in good condition. We can go get it right now."

"Yea!" cried Caleb.

"God provided a bike!" exclaimed Cassie.

When Caleb saw the bike, he could hardly believe his eyes. It was even cooler than the bike that had been stolen.

On the way home Caleb said, "Dad, do you remember that you told me that you would be even sadder if I stole from someone else? I keep thinking about that. Can we pray for the person who stole my bike?"

Let's Talk

1. What are some ways Caleb glorified God in this story?

2. What did Cassie do that glorified God?

3. What did Caleb's dad say would make him sadder than having the bike stolen?

Let's Pray

I will praise you, O Lord my God, with all my heart; I will glorify your name forever. (PSALM 86:12)

Make this verse your prayer.

Q. What is the ninth commandment?

A. "You shall not give false testimony against your neighbor" (Exodus 20:16).

Q. What does the ninth commandment teach you?

A. To tell the truth at all times.

The Pine Car Derby

Caleb was hard at work in the garage when Angus and Daniel came walking in. "Hey, Caleb, what are you doing?" asked Daniel.

"I'm working on the Silver Lightning," replied Caleb.

"What's that?" asked Daniel.

"The Silver Lightning is the car that's going to win the Pine Car Derby at church next Wednesday night," Caleb proudly announced.

"Oh, how wrong you are," said Daniel with a big grin. "The winner will be my Purple #3 Super-Modified Speed Mobile!"

Angus could not keep quiet any longer. "Guys, you're both wrong. My car is going to win, and it's going to win without one of those special names. You can just forget about that race—I've already won it!" he boasted.

After Angus left, Caleb said, "I wonder why Angus is so sure he'll win the race? I'll bet his dad is helping him, and that's against the rules."

The boys didn't see much of each other that week. They were working on their pine cars. Finally the big day arrived. All three boys came early to test their cars. On the registration table stood three trophies—one for third place, a bigger one for second place, and a really big trophy for first place. The boys stood and stared at the shiny trophies. Each of them really wanted one.

"Come on, kids, line up so the racing can begin," called Mr. Grant.

Angus, Caleb, and Daniel all made it to the second round, but then Caleb lost. "I'm sorry you lost," said Daniel.

"That's okay," said Caleb. "I had fun anyway."

Shortly after that, Daniel's car lost, and he was out of the race. He was really upset. "Come on, Daniel," urged Caleb. "Angus hasn't been eliminated yet. Let's go watch him race."

"I don't want to watch that cheater," Daniel muttered as he walked away.

Soon there were only four cars left. One belonged to Angus, one belonged to a girl, and two belonged to older boys. After a couple more races, one of the older boys was eliminated. The excitement mounted. Everyone crowded around to see who would win. Zoom went the cars. The girl's car crossed the finish line first, then Angus's car, and then the older boy's car. Everyone clapped as the three of them received their trophies.

Everyone, that is, except Daniel. "Angus cheated," Daniel said to the kids standing around him.

"What do you mean?" asked one of the kids.

"His dad helped him," replied Daniel as he left to go home.

The word spread fast, and soon all the kids were grumbling. The older boy who lost the race was really mad. He went to Mr. Grant and told him that Angus had cheated.

"I don't think Angus would do that," said Mr. Grant, "but I'll look into it."

Mr. Grant found Angus and asked him if his dad had helped him. "No, sir," said Angus. "That's against the rules." Angus's dad walked up and Angus said, "Dad, tell Mr. Grant that you didn't help me."

"Angus, I didn't think you would do that, but I had to ask since someone reported it. I'm really sorry that such an awful rumor got started."

Then Mr. Grant talked to the other kids until he found out how it all started.

When he talked to Daniel, he asked him why he said such a terrible thing about his friend. "I thought it was true," said Daniel. "Caleb told me."

Then Mr. Grant talked to Caleb, who said, "Oh no, I was just kidding. I didn't think Daniel would take it seriously."

"Boys," said Mr. Grant, "do you realize that you broke the ninth commandment by giving false testimony against your friend? This really hurt Angus. What do you think you should do?"

"We need to ask the Lord to forgive us," said Caleb.

"And we need to ask Angus to forgive us," said Daniel.

"That's right, boys, and I think there's something else you must do. You need to tell the other kids what you've done so they won't think that Angus cheated. I know that will be hard, but it's very important for you to realize how harmful it is to say things that are untrue about someone else. You may think it won't matter, but it does."

Let's Talk

1. After Daniel and Caleb broke the ninth commandment, what are some things they could do to glorify God?

2. How can Angus glorify God?

3. What did you learn from this story?

Let's Pray

I will praise you, O Lord my God, with all my heart; I will glorify your name forever. (Psalm 86:12)

Make this verse your prayer.

Q. What is the tenth commandment?

A. "You shall not covet your neighbor's house. You shall not covet your neighbor's wife, or his manservant or maidservant, his ox or donkey, or anything that belongs to your neighbor" (Exodus 20:17).

Q. What does the tenth commandment teach you?

A. To be content with whatever God chooses to give me.

Jealousy!

Daniel is the city's star soccer player in his age group. Every week his name is in the paper as one of the high scorers. His picture has even been in the paper several times. He has led his team to the championship, and everyone knows that he will get the trophy for best all-round player.

On Saturday morning, Angus and Daniel met each other in Caleb's front yard. As they walked to the backyard for Truth Time, Angus said, "I'm excited that our soccer team made it to finals, but I don't like having to play Caleb's team. Caleb is our best friend. I don't want his team to lose."

Caleb was already in his tent. As the boys crawled in, Caleb said, "Hi, guys. Can you believe that next Saturday our teams will play each other for the championship?"

"Yeah," said Daniel. "This will be the first time our teams have played each other. I feel weird about this."

"Me too," said Angus. "I guess we need to pray that we won't get mad or be jealous of each other."

"Good idea," said Caleb. "You guys know how much I like to win."

Caleb's dad came into the tent and joined them just as the boys were saying their memory verse. Each one recited the tenth commandment, and then Caleb's dad looked at Daniel and teased, "Well, neighbor, you don't have a house, or a wife, or a manservant, or a maidservant, or an ox, or a donkey, so I guess you don't have anything for me to covet."

"Right," Caleb agreed. "But the problem is, it says 'or *anything* that belongs to your neighbor.'"

"But I don't have anything that you don't have," protested Daniel. "You've got more stuff than I do. You even have a tent."

"You've got a foot that I would really like to have," snapped Caleb.

"What?" asked Daniel.

"I know what he means," put in Angus. "The only reason I don't covet your foot is because you're on my team. I'm still sometimes jealous that you're so good."

Daniel became a little defensive. "Well, what do you want me to do? Am I supposed to not do my best so my friends won't be jealous of me?" Angus and Caleb looked at the ground and fiddled with their shoelaces. They felt awful.

"Man, I feel like I'm full of yuck," said Angus.

"Me too," agreed Caleb.

"Boys, I think it's worse than yuck. I think it's sin," said Caleb's dad. "But the good thing is, there's a way to get rid of sin. I'm not sure how you get rid of yuck. So what do you think you need to do?"

"We need to ask God to forgive us," answered Caleb.

"And we need to ask God for grace not to be jealous of Daniel," said Angus.

"And there's something else," said Caleb's dad.

Both boys nodded as they said, "I'm sorry, Daniel. Will you forgive me?"

"Sure," said Daniel. "Angus, you forgave Caleb and me when we said you cheated in the Pine Car Derby. I guess friends have to forgive each other a lot."

"Yeah, the commandments really do show us how much we need a Savior," added Caleb.

Let's Talk

1. How did Caleb and Angus break the tenth commandment?

2. What did they do when they realized they had sinned?

3. What do the commandments show us?

Let's Pray

Be content with what you have, because God has said, "Never will I leave you; never will I forsake you." (HEBREWS 13:5)

Thank God for what you learn about Him in this verse, and pray for grace to glorify Him by being content with what you have.

Q. Can you keep the Ten Commandments perfectly?

A. No. Since the fall of Adam, the only one who has been able to do this is Jesus.

Q. Of what use are the Ten Commandments to you?

A. They teach me what is pleasing to God and how much I need a Savior.

Cassie's New Friend

Good-by, Susie," Cassie called as she got into the car after church. "I'll call you this afternoon."

As everyone buckled up, Cassie's mom said, "Cassie, why didn't you tell Jane good-by? The three of you were walking together."

"Jane really irritates me. She is so *different*," explained Cassie. "Every time Susie and I are talking or playing, *she* comes up and bothers us."

"Well, maybe she just wants to be your friend," said Caleb.

"But we don't need another friend," protested Cassie.

"Actually, Cassie," said her mom, "you and Jane are more than friends. Think about it like this: You are our child, and Caleb is our child. So what does that make you and Caleb?"

"Brother and sister," said Cassie.

"Well, you are a covenant child. You are part of God's family. So what does that make you and everyone else who is part of God's family?"

"Brothers and sisters?" asked Cassie.

"Exactly," said her mom. "You see, God adopts us into His family. He tells us in His Word that He wants us to love each other. In fact, don't you remember that the Ten Commandments teach us how to love God and how to love each other? Everyone in God's family will not be like everyone else. Some people are short, and some are tall. Some like

sports, and some like music. Some are loud, and some are quiet. That is what makes God's family so wonderful. We are different, but we accept and love each other because God loves and accepts us."

"It seems to me that it would be pretty boring if we were all alike," remarked Dad.

Cassie thought for a minute and then asked, "But what if I don't love Jane? She really bugs me. She is so *different* from me. How can I make myself love her?"

Her mom smiled. "Cassie, I'm glad you are honest, and I'm glad you realize that you can't make yourself love someone else. We can't keep God's commandments. We need a Savior. Jesus kept the commandments for us, and He gives us His Holy Spirit to give us the power to do what He tells us to do. We must ask God for grace to love others and for wisdom to know how to show them His love even though we may not *feel* loving. How do you think you could show God's love to Jane?"

"Well, I guess I could have said good-by to her, and I guess I could call her this afternoon."

"Good idea!" said her mom. "Now *why* do you think you should show love to Jane?"

"Because Jesus loves me," Cassie answered.

"Good girl!" said Mom.

That afternoon Cassie called Susie on the telephone. The

two girls talked and giggled. Then Cassie called Jane. After they talked, Cassie looked at her mom sheepishly. "You know, Mom, Jane really is nice. I think that maybe I was afraid Susie would like Jane more than me, so I was being mean to Jane. I'm glad you told me that God wants us to love everyone else in His family. And I'm glad that Jesus gives us the grace to do what He tells us to do."

Let's Talk

1. What happened in this story?

2. Why should we love other people in God's family?

3. Can we make ourselves love others?

4. Who kept the commandments for us?

5. Who gives us power to glorify God by loving Him and loving others?

Let's Pray

"Teacher, which is the greatest commandment in the Law?" Jesus replied: "'Love the Lord your God with all your heart and with all your soul and with all your mind.' This is the first and greatest commandment. And the second is like it: 'Love your neighbor as yourself.'" (Matthew 22:36-39)

Ask God for grace to glorify Him by obeying His commandments.

29

Q. What is prayer?

A. Prayer is asking God for the things He has promised in the Bible and giving thanks for what He has given.

Q. In whose name are we to pray?

A. In the name of Christ only.

Q. What did Christ give us to teach us about prayer?

A. The Lord's Prayer.

Caleb's Candy Adventure

Caleb was spending the day with a friend named James. James's dad was president of a huge candy company, and the company limousine picked the boys up and took them to the tall building where James's dad worked.

"I have never been in such a big car," said Caleb as they rode in the limousine. "This is so cool."

When they got to the company building, the boys hopped out of the limousine, and Caleb followed James through the doors and into the elevator. They rode to the top floor.

When they got out of the elevator, Caleb said, "This looks like a palace or something." He was a little scared, but James didn't seem at all frightened. He walked right up to the big doors with a sign that said President. When James put his hand on the doorknob, Caleb whispered, "Are you sure this is okay? Shouldn't we knock or ask someone if we can go in there?"

James looked at him in surprise. "Of course not. This is my daddy's office. He told me I can come in any time." James confidently opened the door and ran past all the important-looking men and women sitting around the long table.

"Hi, boys," called James's dad as James ran and jumped onto his lap.

Caleb stood at the door absolutely terrified.

"Come on, Caleb," called James. "It's okay. This is my dad."

Caleb walked slowly to the head of the table as James's dad said, "Our meeting is adjourned until this afternoon. I have some very important business to take care of. I'm taking these boys to lunch and on a tour of our factory."

That night Caleb told his family about his day. He opened an enormous bag with candy for everyone. "I couldn't believe that James opened that big door and walked right into the president's office. All of those adults looked so important, but no one told us we couldn't go in there. Then when James's dad showed us around the factory, we got all this candy for free!"

"You had quite an adventure," said Dad. "You know, this makes me think about a verse from the Bible." He picked up his Bible, turned to Hebrews 4:14-16 (NKJV), and read:

"'Seeing then that we have a great High Priest who has passed through the heavens, Jesus the Son of God, let us hold fast our confession. For we do not have a High Priest who cannot sympathize with our weaknesses, but was in all points tempted as we are, yet without sin. Let us therefore come boldly to the throne of grace, that we may obtain mercy and find grace to help in time of need.'

"You see, kids," explained Caleb's dad, "Jesus is our High Priest. He died for our sins, and now He sits at God's right hand and prays for us. Because of this, we can come boldly to God's throne of grace in prayer. Caleb, you and James could go boldly into that big office because it was James's dad's office. If it had been you and Daniel, you would not have been able to walk in without an appointment. You also got all of this candy for free because James's dad is president of the company. When we pray, we go boldly into God's presence, and the treasures we receive are free because God is our Father."

"What are the treasures?" asked Cassie.

"These treasures are better than candy," said her dad. "The treasures are the spiritual blessings God has promised to His children. One of the treasures is prayer. Some of the other treasures are His love and joy, the forgiveness of our sins, His comfort when we are sad, His peace, and His grace to enable us to love and serve Him. These are treasures that can't be bought with silver and gold. They were bought with the precious blood of Jesus."

Let's Talk

1. Why could Caleb and James go into the office of the president of the candy factory?
2. Why can we go to the throne of God in prayer?
3. What are some of the treasures our heavenly Father gives to us?

Let's Pray

Seeing then that we have a great High Priest who has passed through the heavens, Jesus the Son of God, let us hold fast our confession. For we do not have a High Priest who cannot sympathize with our weaknesses, but was in all points tempted as we are, yet without sin. Let us therefore come boldly to the throne of grace, that we may obtain mercy and find grace to help in time of need. (Hebrews 4:14-16 NKJV)

Thank God for what you learn in these verses.

Q. What is the Lord's Prayer?

A. "Our Father which art in heaven, hallowed be thy name. Thy kingdom come. Thy will be done in earth, as it is in heaven. Give us this day our daily bread. And forgive us our debts, as we forgive our debtors. And lead us not into temptation, but deliver us from evil: for thine is the kingdom, and the power, and the glory, forever. Amen."

Q. How many petitions [requests] are there in the Lord's Prayer?

A. Six.

Q. What is the first petition?

A. "Hallowed be thy name."

Q. *What do we pray for in the first petition?*

A. *That God's name may be honored by us and all people.*

(The answers are from the original edition.)

Cassie's Tender Heart

Cassie and Caleb love family devotion time. They like snuggling with their parents and hearing stories from God's Word. Every night when they finish reading the Bible, their dad says, "Let us therefore come boldly to the throne of grace, that we may obtain mercy and find grace to help in time of need." Then the whole family prays the Lord's Prayer together.

The Bible says that God's Word is "living and active" (Hebrews 4:12). The Lord's Prayer surely did become alive and active in Cassie's heart. The more she said it, the more she loved to say it. All during the day she thought about it.

One afternoon Cassie was playing on the swing set in the backyard. Some older neighborhood boys were walking down the street. They were talking loudly, and Cassie could hear them. They kept using God's name in vain. Cassie stopped swinging and just sat there. Tears began streaming down her face.

Just then Caleb came outside to play with her. He took one look at her and asked, "Cassie, what's wrong?"

"Listen to those boys," she whispered. Then she quickly said, "No! Don't listen. I don't want you to hear what they are saying. Let's go inside."

"Cassie, what in the world are you talking about?" asked Caleb. He peered around the shrubbery to see who and what had upset her.

"Come on, Caleb," urged Cassie as she tugged at his arm and started inside. When they walked into the kitchen, Cassie looked sad.

Her mom said, "Cassie, what's wrong?"

Cassie was trying to keep from crying, so Caleb spoke up. "Something has really upset her, Mom. It's something about those older guys walking down the street."

Cassie wiped away a tear and said, "I was swinging, and I heard loud talking. I looked and there were some boys on one side of the street and some other boys on the other side. They were yelling at each other. They were talking mean, and they were using God's name in vain. It made me so sad that I started crying."

Cassie's mom sat down and held out her arms. Cassie crawled up in her mother's lap and felt her mom's arms around her. Caleb sat on the floor and watched.

No one said anything for a few moments. Then Cassie's mom said, "Cassie, it makes me sad to see you sad, but it also makes me very grateful to see your heart so tender. It's God's grace in you that makes you weep over sin. It's God's grace in you that makes you want everyone to honor God's name. We live in a sinful world, and that should make us very sad. But we have joy because God has put His Spirit in our hearts and made us love Him and want to honor Him. When we get to the place that we weep when God's name is dishonored, then we really understand what it means to pray, 'Hallowed be thy name.' I am very thankful that God has given you grace to understand that. Now why don't we pray for those boys? Let's ask God to work in their hearts so they will come to honor His name."

And that is exactly what Cassie, Caleb, and their mom did—not just that afternoon, but every night during their family devotion time.

Let's Talk

1. Why was Cassie sad?

2. How do you feel when God's name is not honored?

3. What are some ways you can glorify God by honoring His name?

Let's Pray

Let us therefore come boldly to the throne of grace, that we may obtain mercy and find grace to help in time of need. (HEBREWS 4:16 NKJV)

Pray the Lord's Prayer.

Q. What is the second petition?

A. "Thy kingdom come."

Q. What do we pray for in the second petition?

A. That the Gospel may be preached in all the world and be believed and obeyed by us and all people.

Q. What is the third petition?

A. "Thy will be done in earth, as it is in heaven."

Q. What do we pray for in the third petition?

A. That people on earth may serve God as the angels do in heaven.

Q. What is the fourth petition?

A. "Give us this day our daily bread."

Q. *What do we pray for in the fourth petition?*

A. *That God would give us all things needful for our bodies and souls.*

(The answers are from the original edition.)

"Maybe Prayer Does Work"

It was evening and family devotion time again. Cassie and Caleb listened to the Bible story. Then their dad said, "'Let us therefore come boldly to the throne of grace, that we may obtain mercy and find grace to help in time of need.'" The whole family prayed the Lord's Prayer together, and then each of them prayed.

For several weeks Cassie had prayed the same thing: "Dear Father, please help those boys on our street to honor Your name." But on this night, she added something else: "And help me to spread Your kingdom here on our street."

The next day Cassie was sitting on her front porch drawing pictures of bugs. Cassie loved creepy, crawly things. When she looked up from her drawing, she saw one of the boys she had been praying for walking slowly down the street. *He looks sad*, she thought to herself. Then she said, "Hi."

The boy looked surprised.

Cassie smiled. "Hi," she said again.

"Umph," the boy grunted.

Cassie felt pretty brave, so she said, "My name is Cassie. What's yours?"

"What's it to you?" the boy snapped.

Suddenly Cassie felt very brave. "Well, I've been praying for you, and so I would like to know your name."

"You've been doing what?" the boy asked.

"I pray for you," Cassie said.

"Well, your prayers must not be working," said the boy.

"Why do you say that?" asked Cassie.

"What do you care?" the boy said in a mean voice.

"Well, I care a lot. Why don't you think my prayers are working?" asked Cassie.

"Because if your prayers were working, my mom and I wouldn't be in the fix we're in,"

said the boy angrily. "My dad has left, and we don't have any money. We're going to have to leave our house, and we don't have any place to go. There. Now you know. So what good have your prayers done?"

"Oh, how awful," said Cassie. "I'm so sorry. I've been praying that you will honor God's name. Now I'll start praying that God will provide for you. Please tell me your name."

"My name is Hunter, but I don't know what difference it makes," he muttered as he walked away.

That night Cassie told her family about her conversation with Hunter. "Let's pray that God will provide for Hunter and his mother, and let's ask God to give us wisdom to know what we should do to help them," suggested Cassie's mom.

The next morning Cassie's mom and another woman from their church went to see Hunter's mom. They talked to her, and then they talked with the deacons at church. The church helped the family so that they did not have to move out of their house.

That afternoon Cassie and Caleb were having a snack when the doorbell rang. Cassie went to the door. She was surprised to see Hunter. "Hi, Hunter," she said.

Hunter looked sheepish. "I just wanted to tell you that maybe prayer does work. When I got home from school, my mom said that we don't have to move. I remembered that you said you were going to pray for us. Thanks."

That night Cassie's mom told about her visit with Hunter's mom, and Cassie told about Hunter's visit. "Let's thank God for taking care of Hunter and his mom," said Cassie's dad, "and let's pray that God's kingdom will come into their hearts."

Let's Talk

1. What are some ways Cassie glorified God?

2. How did Cassie's mom glorify God?

3. How did their church glorify God?

Let's Pray

Let us therefore come boldly to the throne of grace, that we may obtain mercy and find grace to help in time of need. (HEBREWS 4:16 NKJV).

Pray the Lord's Prayer.

Q. What is the fifth petition?

A. "And forgive us our debts, as we forgive our debtors."

Q. What do we pray for in the fifth petition?

A. That God would pardon our sins for Christ's sake and enable us to forgive those who have injured us.

Q. What is the sixth petition?

A. "And lead us not into temptation, but deliver us from evil."

Q. What do we pray for in the sixth petition?

A. That God would keep us from sin.

(The answers are from the original edition.)

Cassie Learns to Forgive

Cassie was sitting on her porch drawing pictures of spiders and lizards. Remember, she loved creepy, crawly things. She looked up and saw Hunter and another boy walking down the street. "Hi, Hunter," she called.

"Who is that little squirt?" the other boy asked Hunter.

"I don't know—just some kid who always pesters me," said Hunter.

Cassie could not believe Hunter would say such a hurtful thing. The boys walked off laughing. That night she told her family what Hunter had said. "Why would they call me a squirt? And why would Hunter laugh at me? I thought we were friends."

"Cassie," said her dad, "this is a chance for you to really pray that part of the Lord's Prayer that says, 'And forgive us our debts, as we forgive our debtors.' This means that we ask God for grace to forgive those who hurt us because we remember that Jesus forgives *us*."

Then Cassie's mom said, "It is also a good time to pray that God will deliver you from evil. Hunter was not nice to you, and it would be easy for you to be angry with him. You will need to ask the Lord to help you to love Hunter even though he was unkind to you."

"But why did Hunter act like that?" asked Cassie.

"Well," said her dad, "remember that Hunter is not a Christian. Maybe he was afraid the other boy would make fun of him if he knew about you praying and about Hunter and his mom needing money."

"Oh," said Cassie. "I guess we need to keep praying that God's kingdom will come to

Hunter's heart."

The next day Cassie was kicking the soccer ball in her backyard. She looked up, and Hunter was standing at the fence. "Hi, Hunter," she said.

"Are you mad at me?" Hunter asked.

"No," said Cassie. Then she continued, "Well, I guess I *was* mad, but I asked Jesus to help me forgive you, and He did."

"There you go with that praying stuff again," said Hunter. "I don't understand you. You prayed, and things worked out for my mom and me to stay in our house. Then you prayed, and you are not mad at me even though I was mean to you. Maybe there's something to this praying stuff. How do you do it?"

Hunter was about a foot taller than Cassie. He stood on one side of the fence looking down at her while Cassie looked up at him and said, "Well, Hunter, first of all you have to ask Jesus to be your Savior. Then you can go *boldly* to God's throne and talk to Him because you will be His child."

"Cassie, I don't understand exactly what you are telling me, but I do want Jesus to be my Savior. How do I do that?" asked Hunter.

"You tell Him that you know you are a sinner and that you believe He died on the cross to pay for your sin. Then you ask Him to be your Savior," explained Cassie.

That night Cassie told her family what had happened. "You mean Hunter stood right there at our fence and asked Jesus to be his Savior?" asked her dad.

As Cassie nodded, her mom said, "Oh my, this is amazing. I visited Hunter's mom today, and she asked Jesus to be her Savior, too. She asked me if she and Hunter can go to church with us. This is wonderful. We prayed that God's name will be honored and His kingdom spread on our street, and look what He has done!"

Caleb had a big grin on his face as he said, "Let us therefore come *boldly* to the throne of grace, that we may obtain mercy and find grace to help in time of need." Then they prayed the Lord's Prayer together.

Let's Talk

1. What happened in this story?
2. Why should we forgive those who injure us?
3. How did Cassie glorify God?

Let's Pray

Let us therefore come boldly to the throne of grace, that we may obtain mercy and find grace to help in time of need. (Hebrews 4:16)

Pray the Lord's Prayer.

Q. How many sacraments are there?

A. Two.

Q. What are they called?

A. Baptism and the Lord's Supper.

Q. Who appointed these sacraments?

A. The Lord Jesus Christ.

Q. Why did Christ appoint these sacraments?

A. To mark us off from the world and to give us comfort and strength.

Q. What sign is used in baptism?

A. Washing with water.

Q. What does this washing with water represent?

A. Union with Christ by cleansing through His blood.

Q. In whose name are you baptized?

A. In the name of the Father, and of the Son, and of the Holy Spirit.

Q. Who are to be baptized?

A. Believers and their children.

Q. Why are we baptized, even as infants?

A. Because God's command to Abraham is obeyed in our baptism.

Q. What did Jesus say about little children?

A. "Let the little children come to me, and do not hinder them, for the kingdom of heaven belongs to such as these."

Q. What does your baptism call you to be?

A. A true follower of Christ.

33

The Celebration Party

Cassie helped her mom set the table with their best dishes. "Why are we having this party, and who's coming?" she asked as she folded each napkin exactly the way her mother had taught her.

"We're having the party to celebrate Hunter and his mom joining our church. They will be baptized tomorrow, and we want them to remember this special day. We've invited their Sunday school teachers and Pastor Gene and his family.

"Did you have a party when I was baptized?" asked Cassie.

"We sure did," said her mom. "It was a big celebration. Everybody was here, including Pastor Gene and his wife because he baptized you. Would you like to see the pictures?"

"Sure," said Cassie eagerly.

Caleb, who had been visiting his friend Tommy, came in as Mom was getting the photo album from the shelf.

"What's up?" he asked as he plopped down on the couch.

"I'm showing Cassie the pictures of when she was baptized. Do you want to see the ones of you?" asked his mom.

"Sure," said Caleb. "And I have a question. I told Tommy that Hunter and his mom will be baptized tomorrow, and I told him that I was baptized when I was a baby. Tommy is a Christian, but he said he hasn't been baptized. Why were Cassie and I baptized as babies?"

"Well, Caleb," explained his mom, "some churches do not baptize until a person is older, but we believe that baptism is a sign and seal of God's covenant to be our God and the God of our children. When you were baptized, that did not mean that you would automatically become a believer. You did not even know what was happening—in fact, you slept most of the time! But it did mean that you are part of a covenant family. By having you baptized, Daddy and I were saying that we knew you were a sinner and that you needed Jesus to be your Savior. We were saying that we trusted Him to one day give you a new heart so that you would repent of your sin and trust Jesus to be your Savior. We promised to teach you about God. And the other members of our church promised to

help us teach you about the Lord Jesus."

"Why wasn't Hunter baptized when he was a baby?" asked Cassie.

"Because his mom and dad weren't Christians," said her mother. "But Hunter and his mom have now become part of God's family and are joining the church, so they will be baptized to show that they have been cleansed from their sin by the blood of Christ. This is a time of celebration not just for Hunter and his mom but for our whole church. That's why we invited them to dinner tomorrow. They will see that God's family is thrilled to have two new family members."

"It's going to be a great party," said Cassie. "Can we take pictures?"

"That's a good idea," said her mom. "In fact, why don't we buy a photo album and give it to Hunter and his mom so they will remember this special day?"

Let's Talk

1. Why was Cassie's family having a party?

2. What are the two sacraments?

3. Who appointed these sacraments?

Let's Pray

For it is by grace you have been saved, through faith—and this not from yourselves, it is the gift of God— not by works, so that no one can boast. (EPHESIANS 2:8-9)

Ask God for grace to glorify Him in all you do.

Q. What sign is used in the Lord's Supper?

A. Eating bread and drinking wine in remembrance of the suffering and death of Jesus.

Q. What does the bread represent?

A. Christ's body sacrificed for our sins.

Q. What does the wine represent?

A. Christ's blood shed for our sins.

Q. Who may rightly take the Lord's Supper?

A. Those who repent of their sins, believe in Christ, and live a new life.

C and C Time

"Come on, catechism kids, it's C and C time," called Cassie and Caleb's dad.

"What is C and C time?" they asked as they plopped down on the couch on either side of him.

"C and C—cuddle and catechism time with the catechism kids," he laughed.

"Kids, tomorrow is Communion Sunday. We will celebrate the Lord's Supper. Do you know what that means?"

"I do," said Caleb. "It's when some of the men pass out little pieces of bread and little cups of grape juice."

"That's right, but I want you to understand what it means. Listen very carefully as I read from the Bible. Then I will ask you some questions." He read:

"'The Lord Jesus, on the night he was betrayed, took bread, and when he had given thanks, he broke it and said, "This is my body, which is for you; do this in remembrance of me." In the same way, after supper he took the cup, saying, "This cup is

the new covenant in my blood; do this, whenever you drink it, in remembrance of me." For whenever you

eat this bread and drink this cup, you proclaim the Lord's death until he comes' (1 Corinthians 11:23-26)."

"Now let's see if you listened. When did this happen?"

"The night Jesus was betrayed," said Caleb.

"Right," said his dad. "This was the night that Jesus was arrested, so it was just a few hours before He died on the cross. He gathered His disciples together for a meal. He picked up the loaf of bread, gave thanks for it, and then what did He say the bread represented?"

Caleb remembered the catechism answer and replied, "'Christ's body sacrificed for our sins.'"

"That's my catechism kid," said his dad. "Then Jesus took a cup. What did He say the juice in the cup represented?"

"My turn," declared Cassie. "The juice represents 'Christ's blood shed for our sins.'"

"That's my girl," said her dad. "Jesus said that whenever we celebrate the Lord's Supper, we are remembering that He died for us. He died as the sacrifice for our sins. Now how long did He say we should do this?"

"I don't think I heard that part," said Caleb.

Cassie just shook her head.

"Have I stumped the catechism kids?" teased their dad. "Listen again as I read from the Bible. 'For whenever you eat this bread and drink this cup, you proclaim the Lord's death until he comes.'"

"I get it," cried Caleb. "Until He comes—does that mean we are to have the Lord's Supper until He comes back?"

"Exactly," said their dad.

"Dad, why don't we get some of those little pieces of bread and little cups and have the Lord's Supper here at our house?" asked Cassie.

"Good question, Cassie. Sometimes we call the Lord's Supper Communion. Communion means sharing something together. Each individual person or each family does not celebrate the Lord's Supper by themselves. This is a sacrament for the *church* family. The Communion table is at the front of the sanctuary. The bread and juice are on the table. This makes us think about God's family gathering around His table so He can feed His children. He wants us to keep doing this until Jesus comes back so we will remember what He did for us, and so we will remember that one day He is coming back. The Lord's Supper is a very special time for our church family."

Let's Talk

1. What does the bread in the Lord's Supper represent?

2. What does the juice represent?

3. What does the Communion table at the front of the sanctuary make us think about?

4. How long are we to celebrate the Lord's Supper?

Let's Pray

I will praise you, O Lord my God, with all my heart; I will glorify your name forever. (PSALM 86:12)

Make this verse your prayer.

Q. Did Christ remain in the tomb after He was buried?

A. No. He came back out of His tomb on the third day.

Q. Where is Jesus now?

A. At the right hand of the Father, praying for us.

Q. Will the Lord Jesus come again?

A. Yes! He will return to judge the world on the last day.

Jesus Is Coming Back

Guys!" Daniel shouted as he ran to Caleb's backyard. It was Saturday, and Caleb and Angus were waiting for Daniel to come for Truth Time. "Hey, guys," Daniel said again as he got to the tent. "Did you know that Jesus is going to come back to earth?"

"Sure," both boys said at the same time.

"I never heard that before," said Daniel. "I read it in the Bible this morning. Look."

Daniel opened his Bible to Acts 1:8-11 and read:

"'But you will receive power when the Holy Spirit comes on you; and you will be my witnesses in Jerusalem, and in all Judea and Samaria, and to the ends of the earth.' After he said this, he was taken up before their very eyes, and a cloud hid him from their sight. They were looking intently up into the sky as he was going, when suddenly two men dressed in white stood beside them. 'Men of Galilee,' they said, 'why do you stand here looking into the sky? This same Jesus, who has been taken from you into heaven, will come back in the same way you have seen him go into heaven.'"

"Man," said Daniel, "that must have been an awesome

sight. And just think—He's going to come back the same way! When is He coming?"

"No one knows," replied Angus. "But the Bible says He is coming, so we can count on it."

"I remember one time when Dad read these verses, he said that Jesus left His Holy Spirit to help us to glorify Him," said Caleb.

"Yeah," said Daniel. "I guess He doesn't want us to just sit around and wait for Him to come. He says we will receive power and that we are to be His witnesses. What does that mean?"

"Well, I think it means that we are to tell others about Him," said Angus.

The boys were quiet for a few minutes. Then Daniel said, "Caleb and Angus, I'm glad you told me about Jesus. And I'm glad that you help me know more about Him. Now my whole family will live in heaven. Thanks, guys."

Let's Talk

1. What did Daniel read in his Bible?

2. What are we supposed to do until Jesus comes back?

3. Who did Jesus leave to help us to glorify Him?

Let's Pray

So whether you eat or drink or whatever you do, do it all for the glory of God. (1 CORINTHIANS 10:31)

Ask God for grace to glorify Him in everything you do.

Q. What will happen to us when we die?

A. Our bodies will return to dust, while our spirits return to God.

Q. Will the bodies of all the dead be raised again?

A. Yes. Some will be raised to everlasting life and others to everlasting death.

Q. What will God do to unbelievers on the last day?

A. He will cast them into the lake of fire, along with Satan and his angels.

Q. What will the lake of fire be like?

A. It will be an awful place where the lost will suffer for their sins forever.

Q. What will God do for believers on the last day?

A. He will give them a home in the new heaven and the new earth.

Q. What will the new heaven and the new earth be like?

A. It will be a glorious and happy place where the saved will be with Jesus forever.

Cassie and Caleb Remember

Cassie and Caleb love to go with their grandfather, Papa Mac, to visit his mother. They call their great-grandmother Great Ma-Mac. When they hug her, she always says, "I love you children SO much. You are special gifts from the Lord to our family." They know that she loves them, and they know that she loves Jesus.

When they visit Great Ma-Mac, they help Papa Mac do chores for her. Sometimes they rake leaves, sometimes they fix something that is broken, but always they have wonderful refreshments when they finish their work. Great Ma-Mac always has a plate of her famous jelly cookies, delicious shortbread, or her wonderful biscuits and homemade jelly. Then she tells stories.

First she tells them stories about when she was a little girl. They especially like the story about the time she made biscuits and put cotton in the middle. They laugh every time she tells them about how her guests tried to act polite and proper as they chewed the cotton. Great Ma-Mac is a spunky little lady, and there is never a dull minute with her.

Then she tells them a Bible story. Her face glows when she talks about Jesus. She always finishes her story by saying, "Children, do you know what Jesus said?" She reaches for her Bible and opens it to John 14. She does not have to read it because she memorized this verse.

Once when they asked Papa Mac why she bothered to open her Bible, he said, "Because she wants you children to know that these are the very words of Jesus."

Anyway, then she reads John 14:1-3: "'Do not let your hearts be troubled. Trust in God; trust also in me. In my Father's house are many rooms; if it were not so, I would have told you. I am going there to prepare a place for you. And if I go and prepare a place for you,

I will come back and take you to be with me that you also may be where I am.'"

Great Ma-Mac claps her hands together and says, "Children! Jesus has prepared a place for us to be with Him forever. Oh, it will be so wonderful! Now, children, listen very carefully. When Jesus takes me to heaven, don't you say, 'Great Ma-Mac died.' I won't be dead. My old body will return to dust, but my spirit will be with God. I'll be in heaven, and heaven is a glorious and happy place. I'll be more alive than I have ever been. So remember, don't say I'm dead. You tell everyone that Great Ma-Mac has started *really* living because she is in the very presence of God. I don't want anybody to be sad because I sure won't be sad. Will you remember?"

Every time Cassie and Caleb say, "We'll remember."

"Are you sure?" Great Ma-Mac says as she giggles and hugs them.

"We're sure," they laugh.

One morning their mom woke them up and told them that Papa Mac was there to see them. They ran into the living room, but they stopped because Papa Mac looked sad. He held out his arms and hugged them. "Children," he said, "Great Ma-Mac died last night." He began to cry.

Cassie and Caleb hugged him. Then Cassie said, "Oh no, Papa Mac. She's not dead— she just started living."

"Yeah," said Caleb. "She started *really* living because she's with Jesus."

Papa Mac looked at them and smiled. "You're right, kids. We're sad because we'll miss her, but Great Ma-Mac is happier than she has ever been—and that's pretty happy."

Let's Talk

1. What happens to our bodies when we die?

2. What happens to our spirits?

3. What did Great Ma-Mac want them to say when she died?

4. What is heaven like?

5. What did Jesus do for you so that you can live with Him in heaven? (See questions for stories #10-12).

Let's Pray

Do not let your hearts be troubled. Trust in God; trust also in me. In my Father's house are many rooms; if it were not so, I would have told you. I am going there to prepare a place for you. And if I go and prepare a place for you, I will come back and take you to be with me that you also may be where I am. (JOHN 14:1-3)

Thank God for what you learn in these verses.

So whether you eat or drink or whatever you do,
do it all for the glory of God.

I CORINTHIANS 10:31

Glorify the LORD with me; let us exalt his name together

PSALM 34:3